The Other Side of Ocean Grove

Ted David

Ocean Grove Publishing Company
2001

Copyright © 2002, 2018 by Ted David

All rights reserved. Printed and manufactured in the United States of America.

First Edition: March 2002

Ocean Grove Publishing Company

Foreword

God's Square Mile. That's what the Grove has been called. The Historical Society and the Chamber of Commerce have historical books and pamphlets galore. Why then a book about Ocean Grove?

It dawned on me one winter morning that the Grove is getting a popular face. One that is being determined by writers who have spent a few days poking around the old Victorian buildings and talking to a few people. The *National Geographic Magazine* came out with an article complete with pictures. They were here a week or two.

I realized that maybe somebody who has spent part of twenty years here ought to write some of the stories that will most likely never find their way into the popular and now ubiquitous travel articles about the Grove.

What you will find in these pages are stories about the other side of Ocean Grove. Some of the people, places, and things that make Ocean Grove a special place. The stories are true, names have not been changed, and the places really exist. If you really love the Grove, whether you've been here a day, a week or for years, there are stories for you here.

Ted David
Ocean Grove

Dedication

To the good people of Ocean Grove. To all of my friends and loved ones, but especially to Diane, Liz, George, Matt, and "Uncle" Joe.

This is the second printing of this popular little book. Since it first appeared in 2001 lots of things have changed but the heart and soul of Ocean Grove has not. The stories have not been altered or corrected so it has the same errors and omissions as the first. The book is now available at Amazon.com like most everything these days.

Ted David
2018

What people have said about *"The Other Side of Ocean Grove"*

"Finally, somebody has told the story about some of the ordinary people in town, honestly and fairly."................*Boogie, Krisanna's Regular*

"I loved the stories; I laughed out loud and couldn't put it down.".......*Westwood High School Teacher*

"If I knew you were going to say such nice things about me, I would have wanted you to use my last name. I love it."..............*Miss Alice*

"I think you have a hit. Everyone here will want to read it.".........*A certain Minister who can both spell and punctuate*

"My popularity has gone up one hundred percent.".......... *Main Avenue shopkeeper*

"I want a copy for each of the grand kids so they will know why I love the Grove..........*Ocean Grove Grandma*

"I have lived here all my life and didn't know the real story.".........*Ocean Grove local*

"It'll sell like hot cakes right from my store. It's really about life in small town America.".......... *Kevin*

"I especially enjoyed the legal discussion about the Gates, clear and concise." ....*Ocean Grove lawyer*

"Mega loved it, man." .... *Matt and Heather, Pathway Market*

"My mom said I could add it to my summer reading list for school. Cool." .... *Visiting teenager*

"If you could have written this book by a pond in Concord, Massachusetts, you too could have been famous."............*Henry David Thoreau*

Introduction

Are mosquitoes responsible for the founding of Ocean Grove?

Is it really true that you couldn't cut your grass on Sunday in Ocean Grove?

Were there really metal chains that stopped cars from coming into the Grove on Sunday?

Do they really make you eat everything you put on your tray at New Jersey's only real cafeteria, The Sampler Inn?

Where can you get the best toasted buttered roll in town?

If you are besieged with life's troubles, do you know how to bring it up before the men of the Wisdom Bench?

Where is the only market in town where it's still 1957?

The answers to these questions and many more are found in the next twelve chapters.

I hope my friends will forgive me for spilling some of the beans about what used to be called New Jersey's best kept secret: Ocean Grove.

The shortest chapter is on the historical founding of Ocean Grove. If it's a history buff you are, consider purchasing Wayne Ted Bell's book on Ocean Grove.

Table of Contents

Chapter 1:	Blasted Mosquitoes	11
Chapter 2:	The Gates	19
Chapter 3:	Krisanna's	36
Chapter 4:	The Sampler	47
Chapter 5:	Pathway Market	63
Chapter 6:	The Wisdom Bench	72
Chapter 7:	The Beach	88
Chapter 8:	The Flea Market	98
Chapter 9:	The Great Auditorium	114
Chapter 10:	The Queen	130
Chapter 11:	Main Avenue	142
Chapter 12:	Timeless	163

CHAPTER 1

Blasted Mosquitoes
A Brief History of the Founding of Ocean Grove

"Reverend Osborn, I can't go another inch. We have tracked the entire distance of this mosquito infested New Jersey. My legs are weary and bumped with countless bites of the blasted insect you so seek to avoid," said Reverend Thornley, patiently walking beside his friend.

"It won't be long now, dear fellow. God will provide. This I am sure."

With quickening steps and a pole of oak, Osborn cut his way through the saw grass among the pitch pines of what will become Wesley Lake.

The Reverend Osborn was undaunted in his search for that special place at the Jersey Shore. His clear skin, steely blue eyes and full beard masked a youngish face. Since his enlightenment in 1867 at a week-long Camp Meeting at Vineland, New Jersey, he had become the vision of holiness, fired by the words he had heard beneath tents and alongside roaring fires during that week of conversion.

"This is it. This is the place. Our search is over." Osborn looked to heaven, trying to convince himself. He too had reached his breaking point, his staff feeling like a heavy lead pipe and his legs sore and tired.

With that, the troop consisting of those hearty souls of the first Ocean Grove Camp Meeting Association fell to the ground and prayed that Osborn would be satisfied with this central location in Monmouth County, upon which to build the great religious seaside resort of Ocean Grove.

The men hastily pitched their tents they had carried for many weeks and had used on numerous occasions at Toms River, Ocean Gate, Ventnor, and Cape May in search of the place that God had ordained as a proper, convenient, and desirable permanent camp meeting ground and Christian seaside resort for the members and friends of the Methodist Episcopal Church.

As the tents went up, each man prayed also that the blasted mosquito that had driven them from every other campsite within hours after sunset would spare this location with high beach, grove of pine trees, and fine spring fed lakes. Each man drew a sturdy folding wooden chair from his tent and arranged it in a circle as Osborn lit the fire for the evening.

"By the grace of God, we have come here and by His Grace, we shall remain."

The assembled group of seven of the original founders had heard these words before, only to flee in the morning from the threat of the typhoid sting of the salt marsh mosquito. This first seaside camp out actually occurred alongside Long Pond which, with Lake Street, will eventually become the first establishment of the seaside resort envisioned by the founders among pitch pines and sandy soil with a view of God's great Atlantic Ocean. A second lake farther south created a feeling of heavenly separation and seclusion from the modern world.

Methodist camp meetings were not new at the time that Osborn came to Long Pond with his friends. Often lasting many days, religious revivals sought to restore the souls and minds of people who were suffering through the black coal dust of the Industrial Revolution. Bound to cities, away from farms, ocean breezes brought hope of eventual eternal bliss with the Creator.

The embers of the first camp out fire slowly turned to ash as the moon shown among the wavelets of Long Pond and the ocean itself. This would be the test. Reverend Osborn prayed one more time that this would be the spot. The assembled group of holy men curled up in their blankets, hugged the Long Pond shore and prayed with him. Slowly, each man dropped off to sleep amid the silence of a mosquito free evening.

Indeed, the founders awoke on a glorious Sunday morning and gave praise for their delivery. Like schoolboys in the woods, each man rose refreshed and prepared for the task of creating what would become America's premier Methodist camp meeting site.

Slowly over the years since the camp out, Ocean Grove developed between Lake Avenue and Main Avenue. The name of Long Pond was changed to Wesley Lake and became a favorite boating site for Victorian ladies and gentlemen and their children bedecked in coats, ties, and hats.

The tradition of using walled tents, as Osborn and his friends had as residences in the early years, persists to today with 114 still surviving. Back then, photographs of somber tenters in draped, bustled, Victorian dresses, and parasols accompanied by men with bowlers and starched collared shirts seem incongruous sitting beside canvas tents. Walled tents in 1883 ranged from 9 x 9 feet to 14 x 21 feet. As is the practice today, such tents offered space for tables, chairs, and beds. Tenters could rent this equipment from the Camp Meeting Association, where chairs were 25 cents for two week rentals and beds, a dollar and a half. Minimum rental of four week periods cost $10 for the month for the smaller tent and $21 for the larger. If interested in mattresses, however, an additional two dollar charge existed. Camp Meeting also offered to assist tenters in pitching their own tents and furnishing them as needed. Circulars of the day warned tenants that sublets were not allowed and that "strangers" would be required to provide references. Kitchen facilities soon became an issue and Camp Meeting got into the business of renting portable kitchen units that could be added to the walled tent. Eventually, wooden structures, containing kitchen, toilet, and shower, were added and can be still seen standing among today's surviving samples. In winter, tentless, those wooden structures look like just so many sheds, with decking out front patiently waiting the spring thaw.

A stern lot, the consumption of alcohol was prohibited, and most things we think are fun today would have shocked the early Trustees of the Ocean Grove Camp Meeting Association. Their austere visages in pictures at the Ocean Grove Historical Society show many of them deep in thought, arms folded, staring forthrightly into the camera screaming righteousness and religion above earthly pleasures.

The bronze statue out front of today's Great

Auditorium is that of Elwood H. Stokes (1815 - 1897). A strict looking man, wide eyes, high forehead, and bushy brows with yet a fatherly benevolent quality, like you would imagine George Washington possessed, he was the President of the Ocean Grove Camp Meeting Association from 1869 through 1897. It was during his tenure that the Great Auditorium was completed in 1894. Stokes, like the other members of the initial Trustees of the Ocean Grove Camp Meeting Association, received no pay for his work but was able to buy two lots which were subdivided in the Ocean Grove Camp Meeting Ground for $50.

The subdivision of the Camp Meeting Ground was a successful real estate development. The faithful flocked to the mosquito-less land at the New Jersey Shore. Camp Meeting owned all the land and simply leased it to tenants at $10.50 a year for 99 years. Without escalation clauses, current owners continue to pay the same $10.50 annual rent for the ownership privilege to Camp Meeting Association. Real estate taxes are paid to the Township of Neptune for all needed municipal services, as in any other town in New Jersey.

Most of the lots that were created were typically 30 x 60 feet and clabbered Victorian structures with wide rocking porches soon began to rise. With insides often dark in the Victorian style, porches gave residents the opportunity to sit in the sun and take in the air. During the time, however, the fear of airborne disease kept many inside, reading Bibles by candlelight. By 1898, many of the homes that stand today were constructed. Outside the auditorium in June of 1870, the first well was driven in Ocean Grove and given its name, Beersheba, from a well in the Old Testament. It and the gazebo which houses it have become the traditional symbol of Ocean Grove.

Mosquito free evenings, shade provided by pitch pines, and pleasant ocean breezes led to the selection of Auditorium Square for outdoor revival meetings, which were typical of the period. Ministers would harangue the assembled mass on the virtues of Biblical learning. The winding paths down to the beach would reverberate with the choirs of the faithful joined in song. Eventually, as is common in all Camp Meetings, the preacher's stand was enclosed and covered with a roof. By 1875, a framed building was erected in Ocean Grove and the term "auditorium" was used to refer to it. Visitors to Mount Tabor, New Jersey, or Oak Bluffs, Massachusetts, on Martha's Vineyard can see examples of outdoor preacher's stands which did not grow into immense auditoriums, as did that in Ocean Grove.

It is hard to believe that the current auditorium with its wonderful ceiling of southern hard pine, 1,300 electric lights high up, and seating for over 6,000 people, could be completed in 1894, start to finish, in just 92 working days. Designed by Fred T. Camp, a New York architect, it cost about $75,000 raised from contributions.

Gaze up at the wooden ceiling. Could anything so beautiful be built today and at what cost? Sit quietly and reflect upon the hundreds of thousands of worshipers who have come to the Great Auditorium's embrace for Sunday services over the last one hundred and seven years and have gone home with refreshed spirits and outlooks, accomplishing the grand plan of the first founders.

CHAPTER 2

The Gates

The Bible teaches that you must pass through The Gates to obtain the Kingdom of Heaven. So, too, it was in Ocean Grove.

It's 1:45 a.m. in the Grove. Not even the cats and mice are stirring. There's a special reason. It is Sunday morning. Granted police powers by the New Jersey State Legislature, the Camp Meeting Association has declared that all wheeled vehicles must be off the streets of the Grove by midnight Saturday. The town's folk have dutifully removed their cars and trucks, mostly to Asbury Park and Bradley Beach, and have walked home before the strike of midnight to abide by the Camp Meeting Association ordinance. The streets are now clear of the offending vehicles. All is quiet and tranquil. There will be no starter motors, backfires, racing of engines, doors opening and closing. The sound of the ocean can be heard all the way up to Lawrence Avenue to the west. The world has been once again held at bay. The sun will rise on Ocean Grove, as it has for almost one hundred years, without the secular diversion of automobiles, bicycles, prams, strollers, and assorted wheeled devices, bringing Satan himself to the edge of Ocean Grove's heavenly limits.

But if you listen carefully, very carefully, you can hear the greetings at the Gate. With the smallest of squeaks, the chains are removed only for an hour or so, as the Asbury Park Press delivery truck carrying Sunday newspapers to the elderly, infirm, or just plain inquisitive residents of Ocean Grove, makes its way ever so quietly down Main Avenue.

That truck has been making that trip for more than 13 years. The Camp Meeting Association, realizing the benefit of having newspapers delivered to its residents, has simply looked the other way. In fact, one of those papers will be hand delivered through the big wooden door that is the Ocean Grove Police Station located downtown. It will be hours until after services before the papers will get the chance to be read by the Ocean Grove residents, including Police Chief Kent A. Cole. Wilbur Dinegar and Jean Dinegar will be getting their paper too, checking the local news from Monmouth County's most widely circulated newspaper.

Like a scene from the 70's Mission Impossible T.V. show, Robert E. Schaad, owner of the Ocean Grove News Service, a New Jersey Corporation, knows he must carry out his mission of delivering papers quietly and efficiently and be out of town by the stroke of 2:30 a.m., if he is to continue in the favor the Ocean Grove Camp

Meeting Association. Bundles of papers are left downtown. Residents who have home delivery find the paper on their porches, well in advance of the rise of the sun and the call to services.

But this time it will be different for Bob Schaad. Wilbur and Jean Dinegar will be signing complaints against him and his company for violation of Ordinance 73-2 of the Camp Meeting Association adopted on April 27, 1973. The new law, wishing to make clear that certain activities offend the sensibilities of the Methodist community, provides specifically that:

1. The following shall be prohibited within the geographical limits of Ocean Grove on Sunday, also known as the Sabbath, throughout each year:
    a) The riding, parking, or allowing to remain parked, of all vehicles, including bicycles, automobiles, buses, trucks, trailers, horses or other livestock, and wagons, except in enclosed areas;
    b) The selling or delivering of newspapers, periodicals, advertising circulars, vending of any form of merchandise, including milk, prepared or unprepared food stuffs, except

	when served by and consumed within a restaurant, coffee shop, or other establishment permitted to serve food stuffs;
c)	Ocean bathing;
d)	Fishing, boating, sunbathing, or the wearing of bathing apparel in public;
e)	The building repair or construction of buildings or structure, including the engaging in carpentry, painting, machinery, and similar activities both inside and outside of said buildings or structures;
f)	Athletic exercise, the playing of games in vacant lots, playgrounds, parks, streets, sidewalks, or promenades; roller skating, ice skating, and similar activities;
g)	The mowing and care of lawns, shrubbery, and flowers;
h)	The placing or exposure of clothing, bedding or other articles on wash or drying lines or lines of similar character.

The Camp Meeting Association meant what it said and provided in Section 2:

"that any person or persons or corporation violating any of the provisions of this Ordinance shall upon conviction pay a fine not exceeding $200 or be imprisoned in the County Jail for a period not exceeding thirty days or both fine and imprisonment. Each day that this Ordinance was violated was deemed and taken to be a separate and distinct offense."

Poor Bob Schaad. Clearly, he was both driving his vehicle on Sunday and selling and delivering newspapers. Wilbur and Jean Dinegar would have none of it and a complaint under Ordinance 73-2 was filed against him.

Bob Schaad had purchased the Ocean Grove News Service only one year before in 1972. His predecessor had made the run to Ocean Grove quietly and efficiently for thirteen years before. Nothing in his conduct had changed. He piled his papers high in his truck, drove quietly through the streets of Ocean Grove and exited before the appointed hour. In fact, Schaad had written to Frank Henson, Executive Director of the Camp Meeting Association, three months after taking over the business and explained that it would be necessary for him to make deliveries only until about 2:15 a.m. to serve his customers, many of them being elderly. He said that the survival of his business depended upon those Sunday deliveries. He swore that every care would be taken to observe the Sunday quiet of the community.

On February 16, 1973, the Camp Meeting Association responded with typical Christian respect:

"The Business Committee of the Ocean Grove Camp Meeting Association was impressed by your letter of January 15, in which you reviewed your method of newspaper delivery and the problems attending thereto. They appreciate your clear and concise manner of presentation. Sunday morning service is, of course, a matter of concern and they will be grateful for early completion of your Saturday night route.

The Committee extends its good wishes for your success and urges you to continue the pattern which you have established."

Notwithstanding what appeared to be an exception that had been created from the 1973 law expressly for Schaad and his newspapers, he was now staring at a summons and potential fine and imprisonment for delivering newspapers in Ocean Grove.

When quiet negotiation failed, Schaad resorted to the courts. Alfred C. Clapp, the famed Newark attorney, was to write the brief which would eventually bring down the Gates. Michael D. Farren represented the Camp Meeting Association. Both the Attorney General's Office and the National Council of Churches submitted amicus curiae briefs, as "friends of the court," in support of the Camp Meeting Association laws. What was only a half mile round trip for the delivery of newspapers would turn into a legal marathon, which was argued on October 6, 1975, and decided by the New Jersey Supreme Court on February 10, 1977. In its thirty-eight page opinion, the court wrestled with the foundation of Ocean Grove, itself, and in particular, Ordinance 73-2. At the time of the decision in this matter, Ocean Grove was just being considered for inclusion on the National Register as a historic place.

The New Jersey Supreme Court was sensitive that the community had operated with the consent, and in most cases admiration of the residents, under a Charter granted in 1870 which extended authority to create the municipality of Ocean Grove. It was under that grant that streets were laid out, borderlines established, health facilities created, schools erected, and what was at one time sand dunes and a small grove of pitch pine trees grew into a town with a year round population of about 7,500 souls, most of which consisted of the faithful willing to adhere to the Ocean Grove Camp Meeting Association mandates.

Careful to skirt larger issues of the proper role of religion in the lives of the residents of Ocean Grove, the court found the prohibition of newspaper deliveries on Sunday an unconstitutional infringement of the freedom of the press. While the Camp Meeting Association argued that newspapers were sold on Sundays in neighboring municipalities and affidavits on behalf of Ocean Grove swore that the walk from any point in Ocean Grove to the nearest such newspaper outlet did not exceed ten minutes, the court was quick to note, "that it is well known that a substantial portion of the permanent residents are middle-aged or elderly, and it is evident that many of them, especially in inclement weather, would find it difficult to obtain Sunday papers without such a home delivery service as plaintiffs."

The Supreme Court had to reconcile other ordinances in other towns, where an incidental burdening of the press was asserted. In those cases, the court found that some burden of the press did not violate the First Amendment, but here, clearly the total ban on the sale and distribution on Sunday was more than an incidental burden.

The court declared:

"Freedom of the press is of course a fundamental personal right and liberty - one upon which the successful conduct of our democratic processes largely depends. Any attempt to restrict those liberties must be justified by clear public interest."

The court held:

"Accordingly, otherwise legitimate police power goals, such as Sunday rest and quietude and regulation of the use of streets, cannot be pursued by a means that broadly stifle fundamental personal liberty when the end can more narrowly be achieved."

The court tiptoed on the issue of Sunday driving in its totality. Courts try to decide only those issues which are presented before them and, when Constitutional challenges are raised, to narrowly define and hold invalid acts of the legislatures and ordinances of a State. So ever so carefully, the Supreme Court found that Ordinance 73-2 was invalid on free press grounds, but only to the extent of its prohibition of Schaad's present deliveries by truck until 2:30 a.m. on Sundays. By the same token, the court declared the ordinance which prohibited the driving or parking of automobiles or other motor vehicles within the Grove on Sunday to the same limited extent, invalid.

The Schaad case in the Trial Court in New Jersey had gone further and determined that the total prohibition of driving of vehicles on Sunday was invalid. And further, that the statutory grant by the New Jersey Legislature of power to the Camp Meeting Association to provide meeting grounds for religious purposes and to adopt police power ordinances, was violative of the establishment of religion clause of the First Amendment of the United States Constitution and should be struck in its entirety.

The New Jersey Supreme Court refused to follow the Trial Court's lead and held only on the narrow ground permitting Schaad his delivery of newspapers. But with the issues raised by the Trial Court, the Supreme Court was required to respond to whether the Ocean Grove grant of powers from the Legislature offended the separation of church and State to such an extent that it had to be held unconstitutional.

Waltzing around the Constitutional issues and often citing the particular and curious circumstances of the establishment of Ocean Grove and its hundred year charter of 1870, the court refused an expansive reading and was not willing to simply lay low all of the powers of the Ocean Grove Camp Meeting Association. In legal parlance, the court determined that its secular objective of properly ordering what would otherwise be a chaotic Camp Meeting Campground was within the police power granted by the legislature, not for religious reasons, but for simple and obvious secular purposes. The fact that there was an incidental benefit to the Camp Meeting Association in its religious aspect, if any, was permissible incidental to the secular purpose of the Legislation.

Nowhere in the Legislation and ordinances of the Camp Meeting Association were religious qualifications for officers or Trustees of the Camp Meeting Association designated. The court could not find that there was an excessive government entanglement with religion.

The court concluded:
> "We conclude that a sound presumption of validity undergird, our independent determination from the facts and principals of Constitutional law explicated by the highest court of the land that Ocean Grove's statutory police powers, exercised by adoption of the ordinances involved in this case, do not offend the establishment clause of the First Amendment."

The continuing power of the Camp Meeting Association was to be short lived. A most curious case called State of New Jersey v. Louis Celmer, Jr. soon followed.

It seems that Mr. Celmer was out celebrating to excess one evening when he was stopped by the Ocean Grove Police just outside the gates. Poor Louis. Police officers who were there at the time said his alcohol reading was nearly twice the legal limit. He was charged in the Ocean Grove Municipal Court with operating a motor vehicle while under the influence of alcohol, speeding, and disregard of a traffic signal. The Municipal Court, having been created by the Camp Meeting Association itself, found Louis guilty on all charges. Then, the problems started.

As you can well imagine, Mr. Celmer was facing some nasty legal consequences for his alleged deeds: fines, potential loss of license, higher insurance rates, and all the rest. Where can there be a legal defense? Well, Mr. Celmer claimed that the Municipal Court itself, created by the Camp Meeting Association, simply lacked the power to try him. It was part of an "establishment" of religion by the State legislature that, he said, had to be struck down. Interesting argument.

The Celmer case proceeded through the

Monmouth County Court on appeal from the Ocean Grove Municipal Court's determination. On July 12, 1976, the County Court agreed with Celmer and held that the New Jersey statute that gave the Camp Meeting Association the authority to establish a Municipal Court was unconstitutional as a violation of the First Amendment of the U.S. Constitution. The Camp Meeting Association immediately appealed.

In the next court battle, Celmer's case was argued before the New Jersey Superior Court on November 22, 1977 and decided on March 10, 1978. Camp Meeting Association was vindicated, the court holding, following the Schaad case, that all was fine with the Grove's system of government and that the County Court had erroneously decided that the Municipal Court was unconstitutionally created. It was now Celmer's chance to appeal, and that's when the dam burst.

On June 21, 1979, the New Jersey Supreme Court decided Celmer's appeal.

> The court declared:
> "Regardless, however, of the precise phraseology that one utilizes to describe this First Amendment mandate, there can be no question but that at a

minimum it precludes a state from ceding governmental powers to a religious organization ... the Ocean Grove Camp Meeting Association of the United Methodist Church is first and foremost a religious organization."

"In effect, the Legislature has decreed that in Ocean Grove the Church shall be the State and the State shall be the Church. Such a fusion of secular and church power not only violates both the letter and spirit of the First Amendment, it also runs afoul of the establishment clause of our State Constitution."

And then the Court, in just sixty-seven words, changed everything:

"The Ocean Grove Camp Meeting Association of the United Methodist Church can be delegated neither the power to manage public highways or other public property, the power to make laws, nor the power to enforce Board rules through establishment of a police department and municipal court. These functions must hence forth be exercised by the governing body of Neptune Township, of which

Ocean Grove forms a part."

The Supreme Court knew that it had unraveled a social fabric of religious harmony when it said those words and, uncharacteristically for any court, virtually apologized for its action in the last paragraphs of its lengthy opinion:

"In closing, we wish to emphasize that our holding today should not be read as impugning the integrity of either the Association's Board of Trustees or the way of life it has sought to institutionalize in Ocean Grove. We have no doubt that the Board has worked long and hard to establish rules which it earnestly feels will best secure peace, happiness, and tranquility for the community's inhabitants. The administration of the camp grounds has earned the admiration of many citizens and public officials. Indeed, Ocean Grove is now enrolled in the National Registry of Historic Places.

"This way of life need not be abandoned on account of today's decision. The Association may continue to adopt rules which it deems necessary to protect

Ocean Grove's unique cultural and spiritual characteristics. The inhabitants of Ocean Grove, and indeed all others who so choose, remain free to voluntarily abide by those rules ...."

Despite the court's remarks, even the later attempt by the Association to regulate Sunday parking was eventually struck down as well.

And, so it was that Ocean Grove entered into a sometimes uncomfortable marriage with Neptune Township. Since 1979, Neptune has assumed the duties the Camp Meeting Association once had.

The beach still remains the ownership of the Camp Meeting Association, and Sunday closing and prohibition against bathing and sunbathing still exist until 12:30. Not as part of an ordinance providing fines, imprisonment or both, but merely a tradition that has survived more than 125 years. Newspapers have never been more plentiful. Stacks of them are available at Kevin's Stationery Store every morning as the sun rises over quiet and tranquil Ocean Grove.

The chains are now long gone. The brick gate

columns at the top of Main Avenue and the empty guard house set off in the bushes are all that remain of the attempt to keep the Grove separate and apart from the world beyond.

CHAPTER 3

Krisanna's

"I ain't puttin' your turkey in my microwave oven."

"Oh, come on, Jeanie. It'll be good." That's Jimbo, about seventy years old, blue eyes twinkling, red knit hat, beat up tan overcoat from the second time around store.

"You want that damn turkey cooked, you go see Kevin." Jeanie takes no prisoners. During the week, she works in the Asbury Park Schools and on the weekends, here in the café. Jimbo quietly shuffles off for a few minutes and returns with word from Kevin.

"Kevin says that I should take the turkey home and see if somebody in my boarding house can cook it for me. I was just thinking that I'd share it with all of you."

"That's right nice of you, Jimbo. But we can't go cooking turkeys around here. Don't we have enough problems cooking what we're supposed to be cooking; eggs and ham and pork roll and hot dogs? Where would I go find the time to be cooking your turkey, and besides, the thing won't fit," Jeanie says, straightening up the tiny counter behind her.

By this time, Elmer, Ocean Grove's official unofficial security guard, has shuffled up the alley way between Freedman's Bakery and Kevin's Stationery Store and pushed open the much used door of Krisanna's Café. With him, Jeanie, Robert, Boogie, Miss Alice, and me squeezed over in the corner; there's not much room left of the ten by twelve square. Elmer's got his usual outfit on: baseball cap that says "Security" on it, his blue waistcoat, just like real security officers wear with medals draped over his heart, several of them. One says "Sheriff." He's carrying his radio and if you were new to town, you'd swear he was actually somebody on the police or security force. He does do some work with the Ocean Grove Citizen Patrol, but this is his daily get up. Like Jimbo, Elmer is seventy plus himself, a sweet face, missing all of his teeth, with a spry walk from hours of voluntarily patrolling the streets.

Robert pipes up, "Jimbo found a twenty-five pound frozen turkey out front of the Provident Savings Bank right there on Main Avenue."

He puts another three minutes on the microwave, giving a good blast to the pork roll and scrambled eggs that Miss Alice has ordered. Looking up at the ceiling, he sing songs, "What the devil is a frozen turkey doing sitting out front of the bank?"

"Amazing I didn't see it first," Elmer says under his breath, as he sips a coffee from a large paper coffee cup.

Jimbo didn't care how it got there. He picked it up and thanked God for his good luck. He took it over to Krisanna's, where Jeanie and Robert slop butter on my toasted rolls. First he figured he'd try to sell it. So, during the day, anyone that came in was asked if they would like to acquire a frozen turkey. There were no takers. The new crowd that inhabits Ocean Grove still have their own useless frozen turkeys in their freezers from the last holiday giveaway at the local supermarket. Besides, the frozen buzzard carried a label that said "best if used by December 1999."

There are only two tables in Krisanna's. They are the big plastic kind you see on sale at Walmart all the time, with a hole in the middle for an umbrella. Miss Alice is sitting over at one and Boogie is at the other. Miss Alice is dressed in her Sunday finest. A Sunday, going to church meeting chapeau, a fine "Republican" wool coat, matching shoes, and, of course, stockings and heels. She's sitting waiting for that scrambled egg sandwich that Robert is doing up. She's got the look of royalty, clear blue eyes on fleckless pink skin. Her blue veins visible clear down to her well-manicured fingernails.

"Jimbo, you can't cook a turkey in a microwave oven," Miss Alice says. "You've gotta stick it in an oven and roast it proper."

Jimbo accepts his defeat, "I'll just take it home with me then. I didn't mean to cause no problem. Kevin says it should still be good but that people around here won't be buying it because it's too old."

Boogie chimes in, "Take that thing home with you. Let em pop it in the oven back at your old rooming house there in Asbury and throw yourself a summertime Thanksgiving dinner."

Boogie is a handsome devil, curly gray hair, craggy face like a Western movie star, "I've gotta be going soon Jimbo; so, if you need me, I'll help you drag it back. I've got that job today. These guys wanna start at 9:30. What kind of job is that? I've been sitting here since 6:00. It's too warm for the cement. It's too cold for the cement. It's too dry for the cement. It's too wet for the cement. These people make me laugh. I go ahead and round up ten guys to do this job. Ten bucks an hour, and when do they wanna start? 9:30. It makes me laugh."

Boogie is a dance man. That's how he got his name. He's swept his share of lovelies off their feet. He's sitting there with a brown felt hat with the brim turned up.

"Yeah, these people, they always be making me laugh," Robert says, his back to the assembled crew, always having a word of wisdom or two, even though most times it's interrupted by Jeanie. It's a Burns and Allen show every single morning.

"Robert, you be getting out of my way," Jeanie shoves Robert lovingly as she slops the butter good on my burnt buttered roll. She can always tell when my roll is done just the way I like it. The tiny coffee shop fills with smoke. Nobody seems to care. The chatter goes on as usual.

"Jimbo, I'm gonna write this story about that damn turkey of yours," I said.

"Go ahead," he says, "see if I care." He smiles and all the lines in his face seem to be connected to each other.

The bird eventually got back with Jimbo to his rooming house in Asbury Park, and his landlady was kind enough to pop it in a proper oven. Twenty people partook in that summertime Thanksgiving last year.

Kevin owns the building and the coffee shop around back of his stationery store. There's an office in front alongside the store which used to be the real estate office of Bronson and Blair. It's rented now by Lenny Steen. Lenny and his friends were the spark plugs for the real estate revolution in the Grove. Lenny's office window looks out on Main Avenue and shares a common stoop with Kevin's stationery store. Sitting in that office looking out the window most times of day, but especially in the morning, you can see the lost participants in the boom times in Ocean Grove. Guys standing out front, smoking cigarettes, sweeping up debris, working for Kevin, maybe packing or unpacking papers, trying to make a small life for themselves. You'll see the women with saucer eyes, who spend the rest of their day hanging out at the Great Auditorium feeding peanuts to the squirrels. Killing time. Waiting for the next check. Living in rooms along now famous Ocean Pathway. They all have stories. Vaudeville, Broadway, industry, government, and the military, but they keep quiet and shuffle about, biding their remaining days in the sun.

Their individual names aren't important, because they come and go. Some are ex-mental patients released to halfway houses, boarding houses or apartments, where, with a little medication, they stabilize themselves well enough to fit in. Others are just drifters stopping here on the way to the next place. The people with the fancy gingerbread on their houses and pavers in their gardens that cost $2 each pretend they are invisible most times, unless they are complaining to Kevin for giving them a place to rest and socialize. Kevin and I have known each other for years.

"Can you believe this crap, Ted," Kevin says. "They want me to take away the bench out front because it's turning into a hangout."

Kevin and I have been joking about the condition here in the new "Spring Lake" of Monmouth County. For those who have never been to Spring Lake, it is perhaps the loveliest town in New Jersey. Maybe in the country. Maybe in the world. Everything is right and proper there. Clean as a whistle. Expensive as hell. "The Irish Riviera," the t-shirts say. Homogenous, white, upper crust. Kids with braces and Mom's with blunt cut hairdos in mini-vans, arranging play dates.

"Kevin, I worry about things here. How much longer can they have? Rents in the Grove are skyrocketing."

"There have been complaints against me for hiring these guys. Imagine that. That's some Christian attitude," Kevin says, as he smiles and hands a customer her change.

The Grove has been found. *The New York Times* Travel Section must carry a dozen articles each summer. The whole business of the gates and the gingerbread and the quietness, tranquility, and the restful spot for Methodists and their friends have been beaten to death over the last five years.

The Grove was near collapse in the 70's, when its most northerly neighbor, Asbury Park, was still seething with racial strife from the 60's. Soon tourists stopped coming to Asbury. People avoided the Grove, too, worried about its uncomfortable closeness to what could be a racial powder keg. Asbury bottomed out with a downtown that looks like a war zone and is yet to return, though the economic boom is finally reaching there, too. The area around Sunset Lake has been gobbled up by people, restoring and giving life once again to that part of town.

In the 80's, they were giving away houses in the Grove, dilapidated Victorians with tiny dark rooms and floors at forty-five degree angles. Only a fool would be acquiring one of these houses set in sand on brick foundations you could put your finger through. But by the 90's, buyers came from New York and the wealthy counties of North Jersey, pockets stuffed with cash from swollen stock market gains. Knowing a good realtor in town became the only way to get the lowdown on the little old lady who just died on Abbott Avenue without any beneficiaries. Lord knows the number of deals the real estate people made for themselves. Nobody talks about that these days. They just all look prosperous. Those "fools" who bought a handful of those old Victorians are rich now.

The economic boom of the last ten years has led to what you see about you today. Fine restored Victorian homes. Some from the ground up, literally. A few have been joined to their neighbors, creating for this little Hamlet, massive seaside structures.

The *National Geographic* magazine recently sent a photographer and a writer to take a look around Ocean Grove. The old ladies that gave the Grove its once deserved nickname Ocean Grave are fast disappearing. "From Ocean Grave to Ocean Groove," my friend George told the writer. Real estate that you couldn't give away is now a must have at any price.

There are no bars in Ocean Grove. You can't buy liquor by the glass or bottle anywhere. There are no corner pubs where the locals meet to swap stories. Places like Krisanna's and Kevin's Stationery Store fill the void.

At one time the good people of Ocean Grove were all Christians. All similarly situated. All devout in their faith and the purpose of their community. Things are changing. The place has been gentrified. The Grove has been renewed, but not without a price. It won't be long before a guy can't find a single frozen turkey on Main Avenue.

CHAPTER 4

The Sampler

"What would you be having?" said Leroy.

"What comes with the ham?" a lady asks, pushing a brown serving tray along the chrome guide rail, barely able to see over the glass and chrome display case behind which Leroy and his buddy, Al, stand in white crisp uniforms, like servers at a fancy restaurant, their foreheads soaked with perspiration dripping down their shiny black faces.

"Nothing comes with the ham, ma'am, but you could have whatever you want," said Al, ready to scoop up the collard greens or creamed spinach or stewed tomatoes, once the slightest indication is given by the patron by a flick of the wrist or a pointing of a bent aged finger.

The decision on selecting the vegetable that will accompany the ham that Tom Rechlin has carefully sliced off its gigantic bone only moments before, requires careful consideration. Like picking the doctor who is going to do your hip replacement. So many choices. So little time. And after all, she's not all that hungry to begin with.

From her position in the line, she can see at least a dozen different choices, some unrecognizable mush oozing butter and beginning to crisp at the edge from the heat lamps that keep all of the food warm at the Sampler Inn.

It's been this way since 1916. New Jersey has lost all of its other cafeterias. Places where patrons can place the tiniest amount of food on a brown tray, push it along, pay perhaps 95 cents, and sit at one of the vintage tables for hours, looking out the floor to ceiling windows of the restaurant and inn, unhassled by waiters and waitresses questioning how the food is and asking whether or not they can get you anything else.

The Sampler is on Main Avenue on the second beach block next to the Community Garden. There were two big hotels next door, one of which perished in a fire. There's still a vacant lot that now lets morning light into the 100 year old structure. Tom Rechlin and I talked about acquiring that lot and creating an outdoor garden strung with lantern lights, offering a place outside to dine, perhaps with a three piece band to boot. Visions of large tables under the stars had come from a trip I took to Vienna, where the Austrians enjoy outdoor dining and dancing in informal settings that would make most Americans envious.

The elderly patron had never heard of collard greens. She instead opted for the whipped sweet potatoes, stewed tomatoes, and creamed spinach. Too bad for her; she has skipped the delicacy of the macaroni and cheese with its crusty pieces of cheddar cheese browned at the edges, concealing a creamy delicacy of pasta, cheese, and milk below. And poor woman, there are further decisions to make. Not three feet down the tray rail is another server, a Polish girl whose white skin matches the crisp server's outfit, topped with an old fashioned paper hat that keeps her long blond hair from finding its way in the two dozen homemade desserts that sit in the glass display cabinet. Grandma is stopped in her tracks. This is more decision making than she's had since Harry died twenty-two years ago, and it was time to select where the old boy would finally come to rest. Meringue, sitting six inches high on top of a lemon pudding base, seduces more patrons than any other item. But then there is the coconut cream, apple pie, pecan pie, and homemade bread pudding with raisins and whipped cream. What is a woman to do? Confused, she looks to the Polish girl for help.

"Which is your best dessert?" Grandma says.

"Yes. Yes. Dessert," the Polish girl responds, her blue eyes twinkling against the pink of her cheeks from the heat being generated by Leroy and Al's station only a few feet away. She's had to deal with both of them since the summer season began. She's from Warsaw, imported here for the summer as an exchange student, working to learn English to survive in the business world. Her friends, one of whom pours the coffee at the end of the line, has told her to stay clear of Leroy and Al.

"They are black men who know trouble," her friend said.

Al, at six foot six, looks like he could have been a point guard for the Boston Celtics. Tom picks his help carefully. He's a Christian man, and he and his wife, Cathy, have given many a job when others have turned them down.

It soon becomes apparent to Grandma that the Polish girl speaks only half a dozen words of English. Her veiny hand points toward the lemon meringue pie, and the Polish girl scoops up the dish and hands it to her over the counter.

"Eat it good," the Polish girl says.

Grandma is almost at the end of the line now, where it makes a hard right turn in front of the big coffee machine. There, another girl, a Russian, shorter and fatter, with more command of English, asks quickly, "Would you like some coffee? Decaf or regular?"

Grandma is able to handle the decision and orders a decaf, which is poured into an ancient looking china cup and handed to her with a cup saucer. This is the thick porcelain kind. There are no paper cups at the Sampler Inn. In many ways, it is still 1916. A cup of coffee is fifty cents, dessert, a dollar twenty-five. A side of whipped sweet potatoes, oozing with butter and a couple of marshmallows thrown in for good measure, is ninety-five cents.

She's made the end of the line now and the most confusing of all events is about to occur. A tall skinny girl, a junior at a Christian college in Pennsylvania, is eyeing the items on the tray and is at the same time running her right hand up and down the big cash register buttons, clicking away madly. Within seconds, she hands a paper ticket with the total for this evening's dinner to the poor dazzled old lady.

When handed a bill for dinner, we Americans immediately begin rummaging around in our handbags, wallets, and pockets to dig up the coin of the realm, before sinking our teeth into a single morsel of the delicious steaming food in front of us. But not here.

For the ten thousandth time this season, the girl at the cash register advises the patron that when she is done, she can pay on the way out, and she motions over to the front door covered with lace curtains beside which is another cash register and Cathy, Tom Recklin's wife. Cathy makes change, as each person in the line of patrons hands her payment for the evenings delicacies. Getting the idea, the woman looks out at the sea of tables, some sitting ten people, others over against the wall are for four. There are no places for twos. Where will she sit? The chairs beside the tables are the sturdy kind found in restaurants that remind her of places her parents took her to when she was a child. Sturdy, wooden, with rattan seat cushions, not entirely comfortable. Behind the ticket giver was a needlepoint she would swear was made by her mother herself. The letters across the top, a depiction of two people and a house in the center with the words, "God Bless Our Family ... Jennie 1893." Along the walls there are dozens of different types of samplers all framed, glass covered, which have stared down at the tables for the last one hundred years. The regulars no longer even see them. The newcomers like the woman are brought back to an earlier time, when children played with string and needlepoint to create family heirlooms. Dad and maybe Grandpa would frame them with homemade frames of wood and glass, some with gold gilt edges, others in silver.

She finds a seat at the far end of a long table for ten people. As she begins to place her choices on the big table, she is joined by a family of six, with little kids trying to get their fingers in the tapioca pudding. One looks like her grandson, she thinks. She smiles. By dinner's end, they are calling her grandma.

The place is packed tonight. The line to get in is clear down the block. Those impatient souls, who couldn't wait ten or fifteen minutes for the serpentine line to wind its way through the big open glass doors into the air conditioned Valhalla of the dining room, have had to go up the street to a nowhere near as famous an eating place as the Sampler Inn.

The cafeteria is also an Inn. There are some tiny rooms above the dining hall, and they are usually snatched up by regulars, many from New York City dragging their weekend belongings with them from the train station in Asbury Park that deposits visitors within two hours from New York's Grand Central Station.

Some have come to the Grove for religious revival. Others are in search of Ocean Grove porch sales. Pictures and samplers worth thousands of dollars from little old ladies moving to nursing homes, selling everything they own, just so they don't have to carry them back the long narrow staircases to their upstairs bedrooms in houses with Victorian yellow and purple gingerbread and wide planked pine floors. By the way, most of those Ocean Grove bargains have been snapped up by the time you read this book. Sharp shooters from Rumson and Red Bank saw the potential years ago and descended on the Grove with a vengeance, driving station wagons and vans outfitted specifically to haul away the treasures found on the narrow Ocean Grove streets. Prices are up, but there are still some old ladies selling off a world of possessions on a sunny Sunday morning in the spring.

Cathy is the only person, other than Tom, who handles any money at the Sampler. Tall, thin, pretty, blond hair, blue eyes, creamy complexion, long piano fingers, elegant, though dressed in her khakis and Sampler cotton twill collared, bright green golf shirt. She is purity personified. A broad toothy smile to each patron, making change, smiling with satisfaction as each patron's check is lanced by the sharp spike on the cashier's table, where it is stored until evening time when the tally of the day's take is made. Cathy and Tom and young son, Teddy, bought the Sampler from Steve, the Greek man from Loch Harbor who ran it for years. Why are Greeks so good at running restaurants? Making sense out of the puzzles of the culinary pie. Tom had worked for Steve as a labor of love. He had learned the hotel and restaurant business in school but cut his teeth in the real world at the Sampler. The Recklins have been tied to Ocean Grove for generations. Tom's grandfather played the organ in the Great Auditorium. Tom is square jawed. A heart of solid gold. Pure Christian outlook. He looks like a picture of a major league baseball player. In fact, it is one of his loves. You can catch him on Sunday morning, after church, heading out to play a game or two in his pinstriped uniform. Handsome, strong. He's been up since dawn, purchased all of the food for the day's breakfast, lunch, and dinner, stood beside Leroy and Al, slicing away at an unbelievably sized smoked ham, dishing out generous portions. Sometimes, special cuts for friends, topping off with raisin sauce for the privileged few, who wisely select the ham entree.

"The menu outside says you have prunes," the dried up geezer confronts Cathy.

"I'm sorry. Most times we do," Cathy, smiling, responds, "But not today."

"I wouldn't have come in here had I known you had no prunes," the geezer raises his voice.

"Like I said, I'm sorry, but we simply don't have any prunes and besides, we never have prunes at dinnertime."

With that, the old man's temper flares and before she could duck, he spits at her and storms through the exit door across the big expanse of the wooden porch out front where people are rocking away the evening. Unperturbed, Cathy rolls her eyes to the ceiling.

"Another day at the Sampler," she whispers under her breath.

The Sampler is only open the first week in May until the middle of September. For Cathy Recklin, that was plenty of time for her to rediscover just how much she didn't like being the cashier next to the door looking out at the wide porch.

Looking around the large dining room, Cathy could see the regulars. There was Hill and Lil, both now way into their seventies, tiny caricatures of their former selves. Vaudevillians that had entertained in New York City burlesque houses in the twenties. Like two aging, wrinkled bookends, they would quietly slide along the tray rail picking up their favorites: fried flounder, macaroni and cheese, stewed tomatoes. A simple glance at one of the attendants would have a young boy carrying the trays to their favorite table over in the corner, so they too could get a look at the rockers on the porch and Main

Avenue cars going by.

Cathy could see, too, the little German lady with the beret. She wears it to one side like a true European all year, no matter if the temperature is a hundred degrees outside. Clear blue eyes, long gray hair, banana curled as it touches her shoulders, her lipstick slightly misapplied, she sits, back erect, glancing neither left or right, paying attention only to her vegetarian dining experience. French beans, scalloped potatoes, a bowl of vegetable soup. It's her favorite dinner and costs under two dollars. She too could be an actress, landed in Ocean Grove from some far away stage.

There's Ed and Gale, over in the corner, just recently retired. Gale animated, waving her finger at Ed who sits calmly opposite her, listening to her tell about what the Home Owner's Association is and isn't doing, or how the politics in Ocean Grove is worse than anywhere else on earth. They are there for the lamb chops. Best on earth. Hardly costing enough to warrant going to the supermarket and grilling them up at home.

A man most everyone knew as "Old Man Tom," bedraggled in a stained and dirty brown suit, crewcut, shuffling back and forth, nervously shifting weight from one foot to another makes his way through the line. Tom is a piano player. He's worked a bunch of gigs in Ocean

Grove at the Manchester Inn, Day's Ice Cream Parlor, and the old Dolphin no one seeming to object to his unkempt appearance when the man could yank favorite songs out of the piano effortlessly as the crowd bops side to side in unison.

Of course, there's me and Diane. The Sampler has seen me through a marriage and divorce. It became my mother nurturer, as Cathy liked to tease me how I had cemented up the stove in my tiny cottage when my marriage fell apart. Actually, I don't think a single meal has been cooked on that stove in twenty years. Who would sit at home staring out a lonely window, when you could be dining with some of Ocean Grove's finest?

Tom seems to dish out more smoked ham to me. He knows the best pieces and searches for them before showering them with the delightful raisin sauce. A double bowl of macaroni and cheese. Warm pickled beets. The kind I remember as a kid. A tall lemonade, the sides of the glass sweating with the summer humidity, despite the fact that the Sampler is one of the few spots in the Grove that is actually air conditioned. That is, if you could call the hundred year old system that delivers cool air through high overhead metal vents air conditioning.

If you're lucky, there's a tiny concert. Friday evenings, three piece Dixieland bands or local entertainers like Frank Rafferty and Spring, sing their ditties as the fried fish and choice of cocktail sauce go by carried by patrons who smile and nod approvingly at their musical efforts. Many of the diners are old timers. Blue gray hair, accompanied by pressed plaid shirted husbands in shorts with white knobby knees, black shoes, and brown socks. I sometimes think that this is where the real America comes to eat. Not the kind of people you see in *Travel and Leisure* Magazine.

You may also be dining with the Fishing Club, founded a hundred years ago as a natural consequence of having the ocean lap at the shores of Ocean Grove, it has constructed a hundred foot pier that extends into the water. It is one of the few public places along the Jersey shore where tourists can sit out and enjoy sea breezes as the ocean splashes beneath them. The clubhouse sits behind a tall spiked fence with a lock the size of a doorknob that keeps non-members out. In order to join, you must be willing to participate in a spy thriller of intrigue, meeting with members who discuss your intentions as they relate to fish, alcohol, and general conduct. Being voted on by the membership, you are embraced into a fishing club dedicated to Christian principals.

Or maybe it's the Choir Festival. Bring your ticket to attend the festival at the Auditorium and receive ten percent off your Sampler meal. Cars with license plates as far away as Ohio are parked out front. Good Christian men and women who will be the bass and tenors at the festival line up outside the Sampler. You can detect regional dialects, and accents. Some swelter in the summer heat but are unwilling to remove their pale blue sport coats over starched shirts and black pants. Their voices will raise the roof of the Auditorium, carrying their praise of God to the far reaches of the half mile that is Ocean Grove. They all meet here for dinner. The family style dining forces strangers to sit with each other; conversations to begin. The Amish family, she with a doily like hat, he with a full beard, looking like he had stepped out of American Gothic. They'll gladly explain to you how things are on the farm in Pennsylvania.

Some things have changed at the Sampler. The story I've been telling you is before Moonstruck and Captain Jack's up the street and before Nagel's across the street got redone by Lenny Steen. Before hamburgers went from ninety-nine cents, deluxe with french fries, to eight ninety-five. Tom and Cathy sold the Sampler to Chaz and his wife. They were from New York City. She took the money at Cathy's cashier spot, but she was made up and in heels, slacks, and halter tops. They got tired quick and sold it to the current owners, Mel and Byron, who maybe didn't realize that the old porch out front would cost over $100,000 to replace before the Township of Neptune would grant them an occupancy certificate. They carry on now in face of new competition up the street, trying to maintain the tradition of almost a hundred years. The regulars still drift in and out for breakfast, lunch, and a dinner or two. The old building remains, the rooms upstairs, the wide porch out front. The servers still come from Romania, Bulgaria and other far away places.

    Some dining goes on now on the sidewalk in fancy filigree Victorian looking tables and chairs, like Tom had talked about years before.

    It's always worth the price of admission to gaze at the samplers accumulated over the years and imagine all those who have drifted through that line and gone on to their just rewards. The big ham is gone too, with it the wonderful raisin sauce, but new memories are still there for the finding and the Sampler may still offer the best dining value in town.

CHAPTER 5

Pathway Market

There's a vortex in the Grove. Just like out in Sedona, Arizona, with the red rocks that look like they have been placed by aliens, teetering on each other. Spiritualists say that's where the earth's forces are different. Where they converge. A special force field where clocks move slower, people more deliberately. Their blood hardly pumps through their veins. Rod Serling would have loved the place for a Twilight Zone Episode. No matter what the calendar posted over by the butcher area says, here it's still 1957. It's the Pathway Market.

On the corner at Pilgrim Pathway, barely one-half block from the Great Auditorium stands a tribute to Herman Brown and his family, who have run the Pathway Market as a local grocery store/supermarket since the 50's. His son wisely married Heather's sister, Alicia, and now, along with Al the butcher and Matt the stock boy/drummer/musician, they cater to the needs of the Ocean Grove community. The place is easy to find, with wooden stands out front that hold fruits and vegetables under a green awning. Bicycles are leaned up against the wall, unchained and unlocked, their shiny baskets ready to receive the market's booty.

There are only five aisles in the Pathway Market, each one carefully lined with things for sale. Each can carefully dusted stands erect like the church goers at the Auditorium rising for the gospel. Rows and rows of hand placed necessities. Here peanut butter comes in only two varieties, creamy and regular. Bananas appear on hooks in bunches over in the corner. People come in to buy a single baking potato. It's a lofty cavernous space topped with a genuine tin ceiling from the twenties and while the wood floors have been covered with vinyl for cleanliness, they creak giving the hundred year old sub-floor away.

During the 80's, ten dollars would do it for the groceries needed most weekends. Now you need almost twenty. There's been some innovation too. A second cash register up near the glass exit door has been added and when a terrible line develops at the one cash register, a clerk will come up and dutifully man it. Behind the deli counter in the corner is Heather, an Ocean Grove Drew Barrymore look alike, sweet as sugar, studying to become a kindergarten teacher. She has brown eyes, long brown hair, and the kind of smile that must have sent the Trojans off to war. Many a young male shopper has been smitten over the in-house baked roast beef when looking at Heather's pretty face. Al, the butcher, stands beside her with black wavy hair, handsome in his butcher's apron proud of the chickens that whirl in the roaster before customers who order freshly cut pork chops or ground beef for hamburgers. Behind them both is the posting that says: "Homemade Soups Today: Hamburger Vegetable, Beef Barley, Corn Soup," all served up in cardboard containers with lids on them that remind me of the way take away beer was served in the 60's. That hamburger soup is Heather's grandmother's secret recipe. Over one of the two slicers is a handwritten sign that says: "Girls, please let the men move the slicers. They are too heavy."

The market sells the supplies that keep the weekend tourists fat and happy during their visits to the Grove, but it is a lifeline all year for year round residents both of the Grove and Asbury Park. Customers slog over the bridges from Asbury through gates that close at 2 a.m. to stop the "criminal" traffic. They receive plastic bags with inner paper bag liners which they carry back to their rooming houses and fourth floor walk ups. Little old ladies push their metal carts from their porches in the Grove through the market, carefully sizing their purchases so everything will fit nicely in their hand drawn SUV's.

The Pathway Market reminds me of my childhood in Lodi, which back then was an Italian enclave of Roman Catholics, who all attended St. Joseph's Roman

Catholic Church. Tom's Grocery, near where I lived, had wood floors covered with saw dust and gigantic cheeses hanging upside down in the plate glass window. One winter's night, a crazed Sicilian thief smashed that window and made off with yards of the cheeses, leaving behind the cash in the register. I was always surprised that the scent did not lead the police pisans to the thief's doorstep, where they would have found him sipping homemade Chianti and chewing on the purloined provolone. There have been no thefts at the Pathway Market, at least none that I'm aware of. Here, anyone in a ski mask is either just trying to stay warm in winter, or is simply a fashion trendsetter from the East Village, smack off the train from New York City.

Herman Brown, now seventy, and his crew, consisting of his son and daughter-in-law look down from a second floor open walled office onto the grocery floor below. They know their customers from the tops of their heads. David Shotwell, beach manager, Trustee of the Ocean Grove Camp Meeting Association, has tied up Shadow, his black and white miniature collie to the big park bench out front of the Market. He's come to get a few things and to nod approvingly at customers who instantly recognize him. Jim Hubbard, former executive for Xerox in the 70's, now truck driver/song writer and Main Avenue resident known as Big Jim or simply Grandpa Jim to his friends, sorts through the vegetables.

"Hey, Ted. How ya been? How's Diane? Hey, let me show you pictures of the new grandson." Thick powerful hands that steer eighteen wheelers back and forth to Nashville, Tennessee like it was around the corner gently yank out pictures of tiny people that seem to have Jim's mug.

Matt, the stock boy, has had various colors of hair over the years. Lately, it's blond and curled at the tips, looking somewhat like a twenty-first century Ken doll. More than one young lady has made the market a regular stop because of him. Fresh tattoos adorn forearms and shoulders, which today are wrapped around individual toilet tissue rolls being stacked neatly as customers shimmy by him in aisle one. If four people gather, aisle one is impassable in either direction; its ten foot length needs to be negotiated like the narrow alleyways of medieval European cities. Matt glances up and flashes his long eye lashed blue eyes to little old ladies, who seek his assistance in pulling the lima beans off the fourth shelf. They love him.

There are no supermarket sounds at the Pathway Market. No bar codes or scanners. The checkout counter is just that. A counter. Marble worn thin by years of customers leaning and pushing groceries by hand without the assistance of the moving conveyor belt. A tiny metal scale weighs fruits and vegetables. It has no printout, no bells, no whistles, no receipt that thanks you ingenuously for shopping at the market. There is nothing to swipe. Credit cards are not an accepted means of payment so there is no annoying woman searching through her pocketbook for the magic plastic money. The market takes food stamps in all denominations, and they'll accept your check, if they know who you are. For some locals, a tab is run.

Customers wait patiently as the checkout clerk discusses the course she's taking at Brookdale Community College in nearby Lincroft. Newcomers to the Grove fed from the pressure cooker of Northern Jersey and New York City shift their weight back and forth, stunned by the lack of rushing.

"How can they ever make a dime here?" Janice from Brooklyn says.

The place has the smell of a friendly clubhouse. Even the lighting is soft and subdued. It looks more like a stage set for a grocery store than the real thing.

Mr. Brown carries toilet tissue just like Matt and helps him organize the display. He is an Ichabod Crane character, tall and lanky, with an Adam's apple that floats up and down a long thin neck as he talks. His brown hair is worn with a strict part, his eyes are soft and welcoming. There is a real but shy smile, as he winds his way down the narrow corridors of his store.

The market is an extension of your own kitchen. It is a comfortable, safe, warm, friendly place to visit, so shoppers willingly pay the extra cents in some cases and dimes in others for the privilege of the experience.

The Grove was designed to be an island, separate and apart from the tumult of the rest of the world. The Pathway Market has played a strategic role in its isolation. By providing the necessities of life, residents and tourists alike can avoid being reminded of the hustle and bustle that exists outside the Gates.

There are no security guards here or arm-folded managers reaming out tardy checkout clerks to both their and customer's embarrassment. Despite environmental ground poisoning out on Route 71 the empty plot of land may eventually bring a modern supermarket with all the razzle dazzle that the twenty-first century can offer. The opportunity to be stressed, bumped, pushed, and hassled through an American shopping experience. Herman Brown and his successors have nothing to fear from the development plans. Those large supermarkets are simply no competition. His store is as much an Ocean Grove tradition as the Great Auditorium. Loyal customers are simply not ready to abandon the hometown atmosphere. After all, in most cases, it's the reason they came to the Grove in the first place.

Like most things in the Grove, change here too is inevitable. Herman Brown has stacked his last can of peas and sold the market to Keith McNally and David and Nancy Richardson. I got a chance to meet David on the fishing pier.

"We'll be taking some of the dozen or so dog foods off the shelves and replacing them with sauces and marinades," David says.

"Marinades in the Pathway Market?" I think to myself.

"Staying open later and opening Sunday afternoon too," David adds.

Sunday? I am at a loss for words. Change. This man wants change. He, like lots of the newcomers, is entitled to create his own vision of the Grove, but some things are just fine the way they are. Aren't they?

"But not like the market in Spring Lake, not that upscale or fancy. We don't plan that many changes."

I breathe easier.

"Good Luck, Dave, you've bought yourself an institution here, not just a grocery store," I say.

Frankly, I think he knows it.

CHAPTER 6

The Wisdom Bench

Wis·dom: 1. The quality of being wise; The faculty of making the best use of knowledge, experience, understanding, etc.; Good judgment. 2. Learning; erudition; knowledge. 3. Wise discourse or teaching. 4. A wise saying, action, etc.. syn - prudence, knowledge, sapience, understanding.

I'm not old enough to be a member of "The Wisdom Bench." At best, I have been accepted as an associate. The professor. The writer. I have simply muscled in, getting my section of the big wooden bench with the concrete fittings, because I have been plopping down on that particular bench for years to watch the sun rise and light the beach with the first orange glow of morning, without any clue that this was a wise and sage meeting place.

When the summer season finally ends and the beach ticket office is closed, its big front window going bottoms-up, looking now just like a large plywood shutter, some fit members of the Wisdom Bench will drag the heavy wood park bench against the building. Actually, there are three Wisdom Benches. The one out front of the ticket sale window which faces the early morning sun when the breeze blows from the west and two others on the south side of the building, one pushed more caddy-corner than the other, leaving an open space for Frank to drive in his electric wheelchair safe out of the northern breezes that winter delivers.

Friendships along the boardwalk are made casually. No one intends them. They just occur as a natural consequence of how you live your life. The Grove gets the sun before anyone on earth. At least that's the way it seems at six in the morning, as the disk slips up at the end of the horizon casting golden hues on the faces of the early morning walkers and runners. Bleary eyed residents tumble from their sacks and down to their coffee makers. Cups in hand, often with leashed dogs, they ply the boardwalk with pooper scoopers ready for the event. The light is clear and each figure stands out from the background as if lit separately.

There is little competition for the Wisdom Bench at that hour. Coffee with a toasted roll oozing with artery plugging butter from Krisanna's in a tightly wrapped tinfoil envelope is the way to greet sunrise.

You will never be first on the boardwalk here.

Not ever. That's because some people live there. That is, homeless. They shift during the night from Asbury Park to Ocean Grove. Sleepless characters. They are always there somewhere. Maybe a few minutes of rest, but always shuffling in every season. But you can try to beat the regulars who will be there soon after sunrise.

Joe Lopez lives in Neptune but he's a permanent fixture on the boardwalk. He drives his big Chevy Caprice wagon, which when he's working as a funeral director, is used to cart coffins back and forth from the hospital to his basement to be prepared. He parks the big car out front of Kevin's Stationery to meet Richard, who has taken his walk, cane in hand, a few blocks from his house to chit chat with Joe about the day's coming events.

"I've gotta get to work early. I've got some business to attend to," Joe says.

Richard knows that means another fallen veteran will be carefully prepared and buried today. Joe's in his lightweight corduroys today and golf jacket. A baseball cap lets his graying curls hang boyishly below. He's seventy-five. I know it well because we share a birthday, July 29th. He's been telling me for years that this is his last year. His karma. The end of his cycle. He's ready to meet his maker, he says. I tell him he looks terrific and probably will live to be one hundred plus.

Joe is a bona fide American Indian descendent. He's got the ruddy reddish complexion that more than suggests his heritage. A broken nose gives it away like the hood ornament of a 1956 Pontiac. He's the unofficial mayor of Ocean Grove, the way I see it. The back slapper, greeter, teaser, jokester, and when in need, faithful friend and professional. He's heard all of the funeral director jokes that exist. "I know they're dying to get to see you, Joe," the deacon says, as he walks up to Kevin's for his morning *Asbury Park Press*.

Joe won't dally out in front of Kevin's for long. He's come to watch the sun rise, to warm and brown his skin on the coldest days in winter. Besides, he'll have to meet the other members of the bench soon to discuss life's problems, Asbury Park's politics or the running shorts of the cute honey from Avon by the Sea, who smiles at the group of men who each remind her of her grandfather. Joe gets back into the big cruiser and parks out front of the ticket office at the beach. It lets his friends know that he's in town. It's like what they do at the Vatican, when the Pope is in residence and they fly the special Papal flag.

You can find him out there sitting on the bench, staring at the horizon over the big, long, wooden fishing pier, listening to the squabble of seagulls fighting for morsels of crab from the frozen sea. He won't be there alone long. Soon Ken and Bob will make their appearances. Lifelong Grove residents, Ken is a Code Enforcement Officer and Bob is a recent retiree from the Business Office. They come prepared with a thick green army blanket from a surplus store. Joe rises in greeting and listens to the morning's barbs from the Orr brothers. They are twins. Bookends. When the blanket is carefully placed against the cold bench, it's Ken, Joe, and Bob getting ready to review the parade ground, which is the Ocean Grove boardwalk. With any luck, I've found my way to the far end of the bench myself. The conversations quickly move from local politics to national politics. Joe's son works for Ted Kennedy in Washington, D.C. He's got the pipeline to the top. While most fathers would never back off from the bragging rights associated with such success, Joe is a sweetheart. Your most favorite uncle or grandfather. Kind and gentle, humorous and sarcastic. The kind of guy who laughs at his own jokes, but in a friendly real kind of way. There is no hint of any financial success that Joe has encountered. He's teased about his propensity to like gold rings with various stones. For a man of his age, he looks remarkably healthy and happy. That is, when he's not complaining about his wife Anna's relatives from Pennsylvania who hole up with him in Neptune and come to the Grove to enjoy a splash in the ocean.

"The relatives from Nanticoke are here," he'll whine, looking for sympathy from the bench. No one reacts. I suspect he loves his guests, along with kielbasa and other goodies they bring, but, anyone who lives near the beach knows the joy of house guests. My house is particularly valuable due to its lack of spare bedrooms and other accommodations. A twenty-year old pull-out couch has kept the long term visitors to a minimum.

Soon the parade begins. Politicians from Asbury Park who are part-time runners or walkers find their way before the wisdom bench. Friendly greetings and cracks about shifty Asbury politics soon follow. They move on to be replaced by forty-somethings from Avon who have run the boardwalk together for twenty-five years. Joe is proud that Kathy was introduced to her husband, Joe, by him at the bench. As the hours wear by, bird lovers with sacks of crushed stale bread deliver their bounty to screaming white shapes that soar overhead. The bench roars in laughter when the kind bird feeders are rewarded with globs of goop delivered with torpedo-like accuracy rained from the sky, often unnoticed. The bench quiets as Mrs. Bauers approaches. Polite good mornings are exchanged as she surveys each of the boys with a school marm glance. She commands both respect and admiration by her 93 years. Her ebony skin and wide, sad brown eyes are set off by a tennis brim. She's walked from Asbury Park, as she does every morning in all seasons. In summer, she's in a flowered cotton dress and her sturdy leather shoes. She looks like a tourist on a church outing to the Grove for religious revival. But she is a permanent fixture here, still driving to visit sick friends and ferrying them to hospitals and clinics. She may sit on the bench for a minute and the boys are on best behavior with words carefully picked. But she will not rest long, as there are so many things for her to do.

"Now, you boys enjoy the day. I've got to be going. Got to drive over to Freehold this morning. God Bless you all," she says. She moves down the boardwalk, the personification of goodness. She casts a particularly long shadow in the morning light.

It's hard to say who the real members of the wisdom bench are. They come and go. Live and die. Joe buries most of them. But on any given day, you can see Earl, Dominick, Frank, Stosh, Joe, John, Paul, Ken, Bob, Mack huddled together out of the winter wind, all either animated in conversation or sitting stone still, each lost in their own thoughts at the beauty of the morning sky.

Dominick was a photographer for the *Star Ledger*.

His interests still include photos he takes, develops, and frames at his home studio. On weekends, he plays cowboy. Dresses up in chaps, a ten gallon hat, and the real six shooter. He and his buddies meet for target practice in Ocean County. The Wild West at the shore.

Earl is a retired U.S. Army lifer. He's of the blackest of skin and whitest of teeth. He's got somewhat of a southern drawl. He adds a mellow touch with his baritone voice and slow deliberate speech.

Stosh and Frank are both sentenced to a lifetime of motorized wheelchair activity. Neither display any regret or self-pity. Stosh has big American flags flapping from the handles of his motorized trike. A picture of the battleship he served on in World War II is laminated and glued to the back. He smokes a pipe and speaks with an accent. Frank's body gave out on him also. He drives himself down from his house in the Grove to the beachfront. His batteries are strong enough, he says, "to whip to Belmar and back." Which he does often.

Each of these men in the twilight of their lives sit and enjoy each other's company, chat about their problems, and laugh at each other's jokes.

As nine rolls around, the group begins to break up. Each head to their respective positions in life. Joe to the funeral home. Ken and Bob to their positions in the town. Frank, Stosh, Earl to meet with friends or wives for breakfast.

By three in the afternoon the gang has reassembled. The sun's in a different position in the sky now as it dances across the southern hemisphere. On the bench the talk is livelier. More people on the boardwalk stop, chat, and joke with the boys of winter. It reminds me of hanging out at my best friend, Don Chinni's house after school when I was ten years old. Sitting on his big wooden porch, his mom clinking the sides of a glass Kool-Aid pitcher with a long silver spoon, complaining all the while about how we should get part-time jobs. But we would sit on that porch and watch life go by. Learn from each other. Begin the development of our own wisdom.

Now the early frosty morning has given way to deep blue skies. Earl, Frank, Joe, Dominick, Stosh have all taken up their positions on the two benches on the south side of the ticket window building. Each man is lost in thought. From the bench, they can see the wide expanse of the now replenished beachfront in the Grove. The Army Corps of Engineers, along with millions of dollars from the federal taxpayers, dug up sand a mile offshore and conveyed it via gigantic metal tube to the beachfront. In the last several years, most winter storms sent waves crashing against the bulk heads, spilling up and over the boardwalk and on to Ocean Avenue. With federal tax coffers bursting at the seams, legislators were able to grab some of that federal giveaway money and turn the beachfront into a section of the Mojave Desert. When the sun hits it just right, you can see the old beach like refined granulated sugar bordering the reddish Martian-looking stuff that was dragged from the depths. The boys have beaten to death the political waste associated with trying to defeat Mother Nature. All have agreed that local politicians had to get some kind of cut with all that money floating around, but today, the wide beach and the blue skies seem to fit together, even though the only beach sitters on this November morning are seagulls and pigeons.

"Where are the baby pigeons?" Earl says, leaning over Dominick to get a good look at Joe's face. A moment of silence follows.

"What do you mean baby pigeons?" Joe says.

"I mean the baby ones, the little ones, I've never seen them," Earl continues.

No one budges. They look straight ahead into the sun, warming their faces. You can't tell that Earl's got any kind of sunburn from all his beach sitting. Joe looks like a brown berry, a coffee bean ready for the picking. Dominick, wearing his porkpie hat, keeps the sun at bay.

"What the hell do you care about pigeons?" Stosh pipes up. He's blowing some of the embers out of his pipe when he says it.

"I just wanted to know," Earl says.

Joe illuminates but doesn't utter a word. He thinks to himself, "Where the hell are the baby pigeons?"

"There's gotta be baby pigeons cause there's pigeons here all the time," Frank speaks up. He's nestled over in the corner, parked his motorized wheelchair caddy corner so he can see the beach yet still get some of that southern sun.

"You ever been to Venice, Joe?"

"I was there during the war. Pigeons there like you can't believe. Thousands and thousands of them. More than the people. They come out of nowhere," says Earl.

"In Newark, we called them rats with wings," Dominick tosses out.

The conversation is slow. Very, very slow.

Gulps of sunshine and fresh air are taken in before the next words are uttered. These men have time on their side. Not a cell phone among them. Nowhere to go. Sure, their wives will be looking for them soon, but they know where they can find them.

"Maybe the pigeons are born full grown," Earl adds.

Chuckles all around.

"What the hell would be the size of that egg? They do lay eggs, don't they?" Joe asks.

Dominick, level headed, "Of course they lay eggs. They're birds."

"Do all birds lay eggs or do some of them have live young?" Frank wants to know.

"I don't know whether they lay eggs or have little babies or if they take them to the Emergency Room over at Jersey Shore Medical Center, I just want to know, where are the baby pigeons?" Earl, who started this mess, asks again.

It's becoming obvious that no one knows where

the hell the baby pigeons are.

"Have you spent any time looking for baby pigeons?" Joe asks.

"No. Not at all, but I was just sitting here thinking," said Earl.

"I've never seen a pigeon nest," Stosh twists his broken legs in his motorized wheelchair and yanks a big stick match from his pocket, strikes it on the metal supports, and sucks the flame into his pipe bowl.

"Have any of you guys ever seen a real pigeon's nest?"

For a moment, the boys take their eyes off the horizon to glance casually at each other. No one has a clue.

"There's gotta be a nest and there's gotta be baby pigeons somewhere," Joe says. "It's just that they keep them out of the way of people until they're grown enough to take care of themselves."
The sage has spoken.

It sounds reasonable. There are no challenges.

"I just wondered," Earl says.

Personally, I haven't the faintest idea where baby pigeons come from. Ever since I overheard this conversation at the beach, I, the professor, couldn't add a single idea. But I've started looking up around the boards that hold up the fishing pier; you can see big full grown pigeons, but no babies, no nests. Where do they come from and where do they go? It's not important. It's like most of the other things the boys on the bench discuss. They don't fight over right answers. That's not what it's about. It's about sharing wisdom and experience. Joe had never been to Venice. Nobody except Earl had ever been there. That conversation continued for over an hour, Earl talking about some of the Italian girls he remembers in Venice, and the job he did in the Army, freeing the Italians and the French and the Poles and the Hungarians and everybody else on the European continent.

Meetings during the summer change locale. When the ticket office is open, the bench gets moved by someone closer to the beach. Now the boys are in seventh heaven. Along with the long views of the ocean and the occasional passing tanker and freighter are the string bikinis and the young moms racing after their little kids. Joe may be seventy-five, but his eye is eagle sharp. They're all twelve years old when it comes to this stuff, giggling like little boys on a class field trip to the museum, seeing naked statues for the first time. An occasional "oh boy" can be heard from the mouths of any one of them. Some stand, some sit, some lean against the rail that keeps people from falling off the fishing pier on to the blankets of those below. They're livelier now. Joe's tie blows in the wind in the early morning when he's got to get to work by nine, or in the afternoon where he's got something to do around 3:30. Working? Maybe all it involves is checking in with Anna, telling her what he's been up to, what the boys have had to say today. I seek them out. I look forward to leaning up against that rail with the others adding my two cents about the world's condition or politics in Asbury and always, always, keeping an eye out for baby pigeons.

CHAPTER 7

The Beach

Ah, the beach. That ribbon of solitude and tranquility that separates the beach sitter from the rest of the world. It's the special place for some that offers peace, quiet, and alone time. For others, it is a joyous playground for running, digging, walking, and splashing. I've yet to see anyone come off the Ocean Grove Beach looking disgruntled, disappointed, angry or frustrated. All seem to be having a really good time.

In a world captivated by computer screens and electronic games, it's wonderful to see people enjoying themselves with just the basics of sand and surf. Piles of sea sand make Cape Cod-like dunes with beach grass bending in the sea breeze. Since the replenishment project by the Army Corp of Engineers, the beach is three times its former size and there is now a park-like quality. Volley ball, touch football, run the bases, and other games can be played on the large area undisturbed by the waves.

A hundred years ago, bathers in bloomers, covering three-quarters of their body, enjoyed the same beach. Up at the north end, the closest to the Asbury

Park border, was a fabulous complex of hotels and other amusements. It had been financed by the Ocean Grove Camp Meeting Association in the early 1900's. Imagine the North End Hotel with fifty suites with private baths, gigantic parlors, and fireplaces. An underground tunnel connected lockers to the beach and a swimming pool. An electric billboard declared the matinees at the Strand movie theater and an old-fashioned bowling alley, with pins hand set, provided further diversion. Nickel skeeball games were popular family entertainment, where wooden balls were rolled up an incline into baskets which tallied points.

The north end swimming pool had two slides and was ringed by wooden bath houses. A wooden fishing pier extended from the hotel, until it was blown away in a hurricane in 1938. Next door was famed Wesley Lake and the Asbury Park Swan Ride. From the north end, one could see the Ferris wheel at the Palace Amusement Park and the glittering lights along the Asbury Park boardwalk.

At the south end was once a large pavilion and changing lockers. For almost a hundred years, seaside patrons enjoyed the views from covered pavilions, safe from the sun, but still able to enjoy the health giving salt spray. Nothing remains of either of these structures but an occasional wooden post still jutting from its sandy tomb below.

During the hay day of the Camp Meeting Association, ordinances were passed prohibiting bathing, sunbathing, swimming, and the wearing of swimming apparel on the Lord's Day. After the disastrous go around with the *Asbury Park Press* case brought by Robert Schadd, and the drunk driving fiasco with Louis Celmer, Jr., the Sunday rules were voided. Today, religious observance until 12:30 on Sunday is simply requested. A polite sign carrying the message, "Beach Closed an Ocean Grove Tradition for 125 Years," asks for the voluntary cooperation of those visitors who come to the sea to await the completion of services at the Great Auditorium before beginning their day of frolic.

Hot summer days when the roads are sticky and the pavement hot enough to cook eggs, finds sun worshipers lined up and down the boardwalk awaiting the appointed hour and then at 12:30 precisely when the ropes are removed, like ants on sugar, they proceed to their thirty-six square feet of heaven. Blankets are unrolled, beach chairs placed, and umbrellas embedded in the white sand. Within minutes, the empty beach looks like the rest of the Jersey Shore, populated with multi-colored figures dotting the landscape. The aroma of suntan oil fills the air.

Can you imagine what effect this all may have on

aliens visiting the planet?

> "Alpha Centaur 2525 reporting. We have again observed earthlings and their summer behavior. For some yet to be discovered reason, when the ambient air temperature approaches eighty degrees, they disrobe and lie prone on the ground very close to each other. Many motionless for hours. We suggest that invasion should be timed mid-July when this condition exists. Over and Out."

The Ocean Grove beach is less crowded than most of its neighbors, but New Jersey is the densest state and, like our roads, it can fill to capacity on some week-ends. It's curious to watch beach goers decide where to plop. Some seem to like the company of strangers, though they say not a word to them despite the fact their beach chairs nearly touch. Habitual beach chair arranging is evident. Some in distinct horse shoe patterns, others in semi-circles with appropriate space left for friends who will take up their specific place in the formation. Some people have been sitting on the same place on the beach for decades.

A lot has changed on the Ocean Grove Beach in the last hundred years. Like everywhere, bathing attire has gone from the ridiculous to the sublime. European cut suits for men with bulging bellies like watermelons unfortunately mar the landscape from time to time. They are more than offset by the tiniest of string bikinis worn by Rutgers and Monmouth College coeds, who have pushed iron all winter for the opportunity to strut their stuff. More prevalent are contemporary versions of the bloomers of the past, one piece suits worn by young mothers and bathing trunks to the knee by men of all ages. When beach patrons come to the ticket office at the south end seeking their daily badge, Janet, Nadine, and Linda feel obligated to advise the wilder set of the beauties of the Belmar Beach less than two miles away, where, unlike Ocean Grove, a Fort Lauderdale atmosphere exists.

In the Grove, a boom box taken to the beach, where loud radio playing is prohibited, is much more likely to play a gospel sermon delivered at the Great Auditorium the Sunday before. The Belmar beach front is lined with amusements, places to eat, and bars ... yes, bars which sell ice cold beer unknown in the Grove. Or they may suggest Asbury Park, where funky couples with purple hair, families with kids, men seeking men, women seeking women, and both seeking each other can have a glorious day in the sun.

The sights and sounds of the beach change season

to season. The solitude and the screeching of winter seagulls gives way to the clanging bells of the Weaser Ice truck. When I was a boy, lemon ice was sold only at corner grocers. Here, the ice is brought right to the place it's needed most. Lines quickly form with kids hopping up and down trying to get a look inside of the tiny truck, where vats of multi-colored ice are waiting distribution. The trucks have ceilings of barely five feet inside. In cramped quarters, college coeds tipping their way toward college tuition, work the summer finding parking spaces along Ocean Avenue. Some say those trucks make over a thousand dollars a day in ice alone. Sometimes in line, you can see the beach pickers waiting to cool themselves off, dragging plastic bags behind them. Beach pickers are kids who take summer jobs picking up beach goer castaways: bottles, cans, straws, and of course, the ever present cigarette butt. The Grove has recently invested, some twenty-five years after most other towns had, in a beach rake, which is a large metal device with prongs that are set along a conveyer belt. As the rake is dragged forward by a tractor, the prongs dig into the sand, lift up the litter, and toss it gently into a waiting bin. Almost daily during the summer, the big beach rake is dragged across the half mile that is the Ocean Grove beachside. But it is the beach pickers that pick up the rest of the debris; the stuff that blows under the boardwalk, clinging to rocks, being wedged where the beach rake cannot go.

In 1984, a group called the Ocean Grove Beachcombers was organized to pay some attention to the mess on the beach. Those early volunteer beachcombers were people like Will and Frannie Grimes, senior citizens by all accounts. Armed with rubber gloves and plastic bags, joined by Lou, Dorothy, Gale, Tom, Ed, and the others, they stooped, yanked, and pulled, dragging large plastic bags behind them, stuffing them full to be toted away by Camp Meeting Association employees. It's hard to imagine that the beach you see now was once neglected and dirty. Through the efforts of the beachcombers and the groups that were to follow, and finally thanking the economic boom of the 90's, the beach looks almost as clean as someone's back yard.

Licking on a Weaser lemon ice and chewing on the paper squeeze cup, seated at one of the many boardwalk benches, feet up on the railing, you can look out at sand dunes planted with beach grass. They've only been there the last few years. Some are from the sand of the Beach Replenishment Program, like leftovers from Sunday dinner. Others, intentionally pushed there by the Ocean Grove earth movers. The dune grass doesn't just appear, but is planted by volunteers and Boy Scouts from town. So it is with the potted plants, large oak barrels every twenty feet or so on the boardwalk filled to capacity with spring and summer flowers. They're the product of the Ocean Grove Beautification Committee, the men and women volunteers who plant flowers all through the town. These same people maintain them with jugs of water on the hottest of summer days.

The real beach season starts on the Fourth of July with the town parade. The beach gets a review stand right outside of the ticket sales window. Herb, a full time lab science teacher during the year, barks orders like a Marine Corps Drill Sergeant in his role as beach supervisor. He's been running around in the blazing sun squawking on his hand held radio getting the parade festivities ready. He does plenty himself as well as delegates. His shirt is soaked through and his bristle gray crew cut stands straight up despite beads of perspiration. He flies down the boardwalk in his electric golf cart like General Patton on the way to the front. Senators and Congressmen, the Mayor and Council of Neptune, the trustees of the Ocean Grove Camp Meeting Association, dignitaries, socialites, and of course, contributors to the Camp Meeting Association all review the celebration. For a town of just about four thousand people, the Grove puts on a magnificent Fourth of July parade. It is "hometown" America. It's Iowa and Indiana and Kansas and New York, Pennsylvania, Connecticut, and everywhere else, too. Handmade floats carry the choir singing in unison. The various high school bands march spritely. The Shriners from Philadelphia with their tiny go carts circle and entwine each other as they flow down the street. Motorcycle drill teams. Veteran organizations. All beating to the Fourth of July military bands. Lastly, the heroes of the day, the volunteer firemen. In a town where house eaves tend to touch each other, hundred year old wood waits to go up in smoke. It is these volunteers that keep the powder keg that is Ocean Grove from igniting. They wave to crowds and toss candy to kids. The beach is alive with the Fourth of July sounds. From everywhere, flag waving Americans assault the beachfront. Tourists in bathing suits coaxed off the beach watch the dazzling display from the boardwalk.

On any day at any hour, promenading the boardwalk is an Ocean Grove delight. Families with kids in tow. Lovers hand in hand. Friends perching on the metal pipe railings like seagulls themselves, the waves in the distance lapping the shore as a soft hushed background to their conversations. People from all over the state, country, and the world. These are the beach lookers; those who never think of actually taking on the sand and the surf. Some, like the old ladies and men, are wrapped like it's November, though the July mercury screams to 90 degrees. Some bring their lawn chairs and set them up on the Fishing Pier and doze to the sound of the waves whooshing against the big wooden pilings beneath.

The Boardwalk Pavilion in the Center Beach area affords shade and benches to relax and enjoy the scene. Gospel music at 2:00 p.m. brings soulful singers from neighboring churches to entertain for free will donations to the assembled crowds. People in bathing suits, others in jackets and ties, all sharing an Ocean Grove memory from covered benches with views out to the sea. The sweet smell of the ocean breeze stirs memories. People look out over the barrels of flowers donated by loved ones who have lost family and friends, and watch bathers bobbing silently in the waves, like seeing an old reel-to-reel family home movie. I call it Beach Bliss, that special feeling that swells up in most everyone who comes here.

CHAPTER 8

The Flea Market

"I bought it at the flea market for two dollars," the middle-aged excitable Manhattanite tells the interviewer on the Antiques Road Show.

Perhaps you have been visiting Mars lately and aren't aware of this hour long series on one of the cable stations. Unsuspecting souls bring what they think are flea market tchotchke to the discriminating eye of a collector and appraiser of such paraphernalia. Long plastic tubes that look like they were used to syphon gas during the 70's gas shortage are discovered to be extremely rare, pre-telephone interoffice connections from the Western Union building in New York City. Current value $25,000.

The interviewer continues, "Where was the flea market?"

"Oh, in a lovely Victorian town called Ocean Grove. I bought this from the nicest old lady."

He continues with another wide-eyed man holding what looks like an automobile oil dip stick, "I think you're going to be extremely pleased with your find. This is actually a Victorian Coca-Cola syrup stirrer. Extremely rare. If you flip it over, you can see in tiny Egyptian hieroglyphs that you have stumbled upon the original secret recipe for Coca-Cola, itself."

And so the story goes. The hunt for the unique, the special, and perhaps the valuable.

Frankly, at one time, all of Ocean Grove was a flea market paradise. Little old ladies, surviving their husbands, put Victorian accumulations on the block for cents on the dollar. A lot has changed in recent years but one thing has remained constant: New Jersey's most fantastic community flea market. Out front of the Great Auditorium on the expanse of lawn that runs all the way down to the ocean side itself are hundreds of vendors, including the ordinary folk like my friends Julie and George, who for $75 will set up three card tables, one borrowed from me, to participate in the event that is a tradition during the first week of June and the first week of September.

The scenery couldn't be better. The Great Auditorium stands as a Disney backdrop to vendors that begin arriving at 5:30 in the morning. They hardly make a noise. Vans arrive crammed with precise fitting Tupperware boxes filled with inventory to be displayed under nylon tents that create shade and a place to hang the wares at the same time. I'm sure in other parts of the country these community wide affairs can be as organized with local police professionals who provide the know-how. Here in the Grove, the job falls to the Ocean Grove Citizen's Patrol; a hardy band of elderly do-gooders, former captains of industries, retired military personnel or shoe salesmen, teachers, bankers, lawyers, and CPA's, who don the garb of security people with baseball caps which say "OGCP." The group was founded by Ben Douglas, a former owner of Day's Restaurant, to supplement existing police surveillance in the Grove. If they're lucky, members get to ride side by side in the black and white cruiser purchased from the Neptune Police at the last township auction. On flea market days, they swing into action. Barricades are erected. Signs posted. Armed with walkie talkies, they strategically hand out parking area assignments, fifteen minutes to unload that van, and then it's time to move on. Like an ant colony feverishly moving tiny pieces of candy, the venders unload as the sun begins to rise.

George has asked to use my beat up 1980 Toyota pickup truck for the occasion. I wouldn't miss it for the world, so I'm at his place soon after five. My truck is easy to see. It's been in the Grove for twenty years. Fire engine red and covered with 178 bumper stickers, it's been crashed on every panel with the rear end chopped off about nine inches from a nasty accident. But not to worry. The truck's gate, owing to the smash, provides a perfect angle for sticking boxes with little danger of them falling out. George and I pile the truck high with his memorabilia.

"George, not the soap stone Buddha. Anything but that," I said.

George traipsed around the country in his youth, lived in a commune in California, planted seeds, pulled weeds, and maybe smoked some too. Never inhaling, mind you. All the while putting together a sound life philosophy along the way.

"Teddy, it must go, along with all this other junk. I feel I need a purge. A new summer beginning," George says.

So, tucked in with the Buddha, are dozens of pairs of shoes, countless boxes of assorted brick-a-brack, albums, photographs, and his portable six foot round trampoline. Like gypsies with their wagon, we head directly into the fray which is Main Avenue and are guided by Citizen's Patrollers who assign me a temporary parking space for unloading. In a flash, George, muscular and fit from miles of boardwalk bicycling, has the truck unloaded and the precious inventory displayed on the card tables. I've got no goods to sell. My garage still houses my mementos with which I cannot part. But among the varieties of things for sale are my yet to be duplicated Ocean Grove collage picture puzzles.

While tinkering with the digital camera I bought from AOL for $99, I discovered when combined with the Power Point program that interesting collages could be created. Printable on 8 ½ by 11 paper with a little magic, they can be turned into boxed puzzles. This spring has led to the first in a collectible series, so the package states, of 110 piece puzzle called, "O.G. by the Sea." While sales were less than brisk, the Ocean Grove Historical Society was interested enough to take one as part of its permanent collection. Apparently, it was the first puzzle of Ocean Grove that has ever existed. While I'm deeply in your debt for purchasing this book, if you'd like to go the distance, that puzzle can still be purchased from the Historical Society for a mere pittance. But back to the story.

So there, leaning up against the soap stone Buddha, are my prized puzzles. Now a word or two about Julie. A fetching example of the best that Gloversville, New York, has to offer, Julie is a full time O.G. resident. Salt and pepper hair, soft brown eyes permanently widened as if she had seen a ghost. She has assembled her extra jewelry, some of her yoga tapes and yoga books. She's a part time yoga instructor, as well as a county employee. So in no time, the three of us are ready for the day's selling activities. We are situated under a big oak tree across from the Pavilion, which is a Victorian outdoor gazebo of sorts that looks like a flying saucer in wood and carpenter's filigree. It's topped with a small dome and has large steel posts that hold up the roof. The Ladies Auxiliary has their displays there, as well as the breakfast and coffee goodies. Behind the Pavilion, hugging close to the perimeter of the Great Auditorium, are the remnants of the tent colony upon with which Ocean Grove was once populated, numbering more than a thousand during its heyday. One hundred and fourteen canvas survivors still exist. They are both tent and permanent structure. Years ago, tenters who came for the Great Auditorium preaching season began to indulge themselves with desires like indoor plumbing, a shower and toilet of one's own, and perhaps a tiny kitchen, as well. But true to the originals, the sitting room is all canvas. The tents are the tough army surplus looking variety topped with a multi-colored layered bonnet called a fly. Each of them in their own Victorian colors. Tenters who come for the season decorate them with homey furniture and landscape their porches with flowers and herbs in cheerful baskets and urns.

The tents look out of place in our plywood and vinyl covered world, but in the 1860's, they were neatly adapted from officer headquarters on the civil war battlefield. Add a roaring fire and a convenient woods for relieving oneself, and you had first class accommodations. Today, they are both a curiosity and a way of turning back the clock to simpler days, where t.v., radio, cd-rom, computer notebook, and Gameboy were unthought-of. The tents form just another piece of Victorian eye candy for the flea market aficionado.

George and I waste no time rustling up some breakfast. The Ladies Auxiliary have their two portable griddles going full tilt. Eggs, pork roll, and cheese on a sesame seed bun. Some fresh coffee, a donut, and all is right with the world. The temperature is rising along with the shopping population. Carrying paper and plastic bags, well wrapped treasures begin leaving their temporary landings to find new homes in North Jersey and New York. Even George's two foot tall soap stone Buddha has been swept away. The flea market has been advertised for months now, flyers around town, ads in the large newspapers like the *Asbury Park Press*, and of course, the *Ocean Grove Times*.

The *Ocean Grove Times* was a family run two page newspaper that served only the needs of this tiny Methodist community for almost one hundred years. With competition from the outside, from real newspapers, it was eventually sold and became a real paper, itself, sometimes now more than ten pages in length, carrying news of the various towns up and down Monmouth County: Asbury Park, Bradley Beach, Belmar, Spring Lake, Sea Girt. Even its name was changed to the Ocean Grove and Neptune Times. It's no longer printed on Main Avenue in town. Dale Whilden, the dentist, now owns the Times building, where the paper was once published, and has turned it into a dental office with apartments above.

Like the vendors, many of the shoppers are repeaters back to scour things that have been taken down from attics, brought up from basements, and dragged from garages. There are plenty of professionals around. High priced dealers from Red Bank and Rumson, everything neatly tagged and set out. Some with 9 x 12 Oriental carpets covering the grass. But high priced or low priced, it's amazing how many things change hands and some treasures are found. Every then and again someone buys a painting, a sculpture or other artwork to discover it's worth hundreds, if not a thousand times greater than the paltry amount that is paid. Gold and silver baubles gleam in their trays like solid pieces of sunlight themselves. Some of the rings on display in the glass cases under the temporary nylon shelters have come from the Ocean Grove beach itself.

Metal detectors were developed during the First

World War to be used to discover enemy land mines. Suspended from long poles or attached to military vehicles, they swept pathways for invading armies. After the war, they were hung up in army surplus depots around the country. It wasn't long until the American entrepreneurial spirit brought them out of their hiding places to find a use in locating lost metal objects. Companies, like Whites in Sweet, Oregon, have made a full time business of manufacturing such devices. Light weight hand held jobs can be purchased for as little as a hundred bucks. What with two or three hundred thousand sweeps in vacant lots in one's neighborhood, the spare change could easily pay for one of these devices. Some of the more fancy types can be used underwater or at the water's edge. Some can discriminate between pennies, nickels, quarters, saving the treasure hunter the backbreaking boredom of stooping for just a few cents. Some people have used metal detectors as hobbies for all their lives, like Buddy Johnson at the Ocean Grove beach. You can see him most summer mornings before the crowds get there with their gold insignia bracelets, watches, and ankle chains. The dross of society will find its way to a sandy grave on the Ocean Grove beach front. Buddy's contraption has a device he slips his arm into and lets it swing freely left to right, creating a three foot semi-circle as he patiently walks the hot spots of the O.G. Beach. Center Beach, where the tourists are as thick as flies. Gold laden. He'll stop and scoop. He's got his headset comfortably adjusted beneath his baseball cap. The sweep can take him two hours or more but he's been retired for years. He loves the treasure hunting business.

"So how many gold rings have you found today, Buddy?" I said.

"Few here and there," he replies, a tiny smile gently ripples his lips.

On one lazy August morning we talk for almost a half hour. That's when I learned about the display cabinets he's got himself of gold wedding bands, high school rings, watches, and alike.

"Do you ever sell any of this stuff, Buddy?"

"Now and then," he says, as the buzzer on the machine alerts him to a buried penny. He ignores it.

Like a true treasure hunter, he keeps his finds to himself. Not to mention the fact the Internal Revenue Service would probably be interested in taxing him if they knew the exact details.

"I just do it for fun," Buddy says, swinging his right arm and stepping back on the beach for another quick look-see. "I don't find all that much." He winks at me as he walks past.

George is getting a little concerned that he might have to drag his portable one man trampoline back to his apartment. Leaned up against the big oak tree, there has been no bidders. But George is not one to give up quickly. As the snake-like line of lookers and gawkers press around the three folding card tables, George begins a circus act. The trampoline set up, he climbs aboard. Slowly, his five foot eight frame climbs skyward. His legs go out from him. Now cannonball, free style. The crowd is ooohing and aaahing. I'm applauding wildly. He's stopped the crowd with his bit of Ocean Grove flea market marketing. Five minutes before, it looked like this was a haul back situation; now the buyers are actually bidding for the thing. In a flash and $60, it's gone forever to a new home. Recycled. George beams.

A stroll around the flea market grounds can take hours. You hear the newcomers making arrangements with their girlfriends and wives. "I'll meet you back here in two hours." The reality is, they won't see them again all day. In fact, in some cases, they may never see them again, period. One thing leads to another and before you know it, the day is done, night has fallen, and shoppers continue bleary eyed prancing around the grounds looking for lost loved ones.

If you've been here before, you know the killer vendors. Like the Ocean Grove Fishing Club, that venerable institution of one hundred and fifty years which has remained a man's club in the face of women's liberation. You can see them with those ten foot poles. Not the kind you wouldn't go near someone with, but those necessary for salt water fishing. Each spring the members hear the call to deliver their goodies to the fishing pier, so that they may participate in the June outing. Here, long wide tables are arranged in a horse shoe and white haired fishing club members hawk passersby in a way that would have made PT Barnum cringe.

"Why this air conditioner is hardly used," says one of them.

"I knew the old lady who owned it myself, "says another.

"Hated air conditioning. Hated to part with the money to juice up the devil. Why, if it wasn't the fact that this was found in her damp basement off of Abbott Avenue, there would not be a single rust mark on it." He points to a rotting crate of bolts and rivets that may have been twenty years ago an air conditioner.

Another boasts of a castaway t.v. "Sure the picture tube isn't working exactly right." (It's totally black.) "But, it's a hummer and you know what that means; just a tube or a dial somewhere is all that is necessary, and it can be yours for a dollar."

And so it goes at the Fishing Club stand. Clocks. Peppermills by the dozens. Snow shoes with dried out leather bindings. Old tires. Jacks. Kids games. Radios. Phone answering machines. Telephones in all colors and vintages. By the way, I got my phone for two dollars a number of years ago. Still works fine. The members get an opportunity to dump the junk from their attics and basements and a day's fun is had by all. Proceeds are used to maintain the invaluable fishing pier itself. It's the club's responsibility to keep it afloat. They took out a mortgage to replace it the last time, when the unnamed nor'easter swallowed it up whole, sending the fishing club cabin out into the drink. Members watched in horror as a massive wave went over the roof in one giant swell, swept the cabin from its pilings, and set it adrift in the tossing sea. Moments later, it was crashed and its innards sent to the bottom of the ocean. But, undaunted, the club raised the funds to build anew and repaired what looked like a hopeless pile of rubble into the fishing pier and club house you see today.

After several hours of wandering, my favorite time of the day arrives. Lunch.

Ocean Grove has become somewhat of a culinary heaven with the four star rated Moonstruck on Main Avenue. Followed closely is Captain Jack's up the street, owned by Jack Green, one of the trustees of the Camp Meeting Association. Burgers, fries, and assorted delicacies for the cholesterol challenged can be found at Nagels. But right here in the middle of the flea market, some of the restaurants have set up shop. So, along with the normal fair of sausage and peppers, hot dogs and hamburgers, one can acquire a delicious scoop of couscous, perhaps a battered deep fried halibut sandwich as well. To finish it all, the Sampler may be selling some of their desserts.

For the true tube steak lover, the hotdogs sold by the Ladies Auxiliary are not to be missed. These are imported. Not from some far away land, but from Pennsylvania, all beef, truly a culinary delicacy when smothered with sauerkraut and onions and washed down with a sarsaparilla. I had never really seen a sarsaparilla can or bottle until I got to Ocean Grove. Here, it has been a tradition for the last hundred years.

What is sarsaparilla? It is a curious type of drink. Its name comes from a physician named Parillo, who first used it as a medicine. It's a tropical American plant of the genus Smilax. Especially Smilax officinalis of Central America or Smilax medica of Mexico and Smilax papyracea of Brazil. It is a vine that has large fragrant roots and tooth heart shaped leaves. The dried roots of these plants has been used as a tonic and for flavoring for centuries. Any drink flavored with the root is called sarsaparilla. In America, the America sarsaparilla is a perennial herb: aralia nudicaulis, whose roots are used as a substitute for the real thing. Well, if that's what sarsaparilla is, then what is root beer? Nothing as fancy a definition for root beer exists. It is simply any carbonated beverage made from root extracts from certain plants like sarsaparilla or sassafras. Well, whether you call it sarsaparilla or plain American root beer, it is the only way to savor those Pennsylvania hotdogs.

As the day moves on, the flea market is at fever pitch. With all the money changing hands, it looks like the floor of the New York Stock Exchange and it's all delicious cash.

Some years ago the Internal Revenue Service attempted to focus on flea market dealings. Agents posed as buyers and sellers would ferret out the nasty deeds. So too, New Jersey got into the act with sales tax agents. But these days there is not a revenuer in sight. Some vendors dutifully collect the tax, but one can only wonder whether it simply goes directly into their pockets.

Slowly, the shoppers begin to wander out carting behind them their new found treasures. SUV's, whose capacious insides have been used for nothing more than toting perhaps a spare tire, are now filled to bursting with the day's finds.

By nightfall, there is nothing left of the one day extravaganza. All visible signs have vanished. By early morning, the sun rises on the Great Auditorium looking out
on the ocean, and the nomadic tribe of flea market vendors has moved on.

CHAPTER 9

The Great Auditorium

"That reminds me of a story," starts the preacher. "Three old friends were enjoying a round of golf on a beautiful spring morning. As they approached the eighteenth hole, these friends of many years realized that they were each one stroke away from playing the best round of golf they had ever played before. As golf sometimes does, it all came down to the last hole with each of their balls approximately the same distance from the cup, they went in turn. The first two golfers, kneeling on the grass trying to figure out which way the ball would fall. The break. The wind factor. How fast the green was. The last time it had rained. The moisture in the air. The static electricity caused by their clothes and all of the numerous and insurmountable variables that go into placing a white ball ten feet away to a particular spot on the vast open greenery of the golf course. But no matter how hard they tried, each missed by inches. The third friend stepped right up to the ball, confidently grabbed his putter, and with the slightest of taps sent the ball clearly to the center of the cup. The two other friends were astounded, "How did you do that? You didn't even take the time to look."

With confidence, the third friend piped up, "I simply learned from your mistakes."

"It's like that with life. You can either make the mistakes yourself, or you can learn from others. And the Bible is the greatest guidebook of all. It's the mistake misser's handbook." The congregation chuckles. The crowd has been sitting quietly in the six thousand wooden seats that is the Great Auditorium hanging on every word of America's greatest living prophet. Author, teacher, raconteur, minister, father, husband, and friend. Norman Vincent Peale. A fixture in the Grove delivering fifty years of homespun homilies until his death in 1994. When the 60's revolutionaries were throwing rocks and smoking dope, Peale was advocating for positive thinking as the way out of the nation's problems. The Auditorium today is filled to the rafters to hear his words. Seated beside him, his dear wife, Ruth, beaming at the pudgy little man with the gravelly voice standing beside her. His antidotes and jokes enliven his almost two hour sermon. The crowd is hushed and introspective. Tears well up in many of the congregation. It is a special Sunday sermon, the last of the season. The Great Auditorium has worked its magic again. Saving souls, lifting spirits, putting people, families and friends back on the road to salvation.

Saturday night was a different story.

"Lightning strikes again and again and again." With that phrase in shrilly falsetto, the house lights fall dark and hundreds of tiny lights flash, jump, and dazzle to the applause and screams of the crowd. It's Lou Christy in his silver lamé skintight outfit. The light show is sewn into the seams of his get up. The crowd belongs to the night's Doo Wop concert. That version of rhythm and blues and rock and roll that emerged in the middle 1950's and has become the anthem for the country's baby boomers. Only minutes before, the Coasters had brought the house down with "Charlie Brown." Singing and swaying in the Auditorium. The very same place where so many find God, Saturday night it is pure nostalgia served up with electric guitars and drums. It is a marriage of necessity. The wholesome All-American entertainment, carefully screened, helps pay the bills for the religious crusade that is the Camp Meeting Association's quest to make the Great Auditorium a holy place for Christians to meet and listen to the great speakers of the day.

The Grove has had at least three auditoriums on the site of the Great Auditorium, but the building you now see was commenced on October 16, 1893 with the razing of the prior building. It is 225 feet by 161 feet and houses 36,000 square feet of space. It provides seating for over 6,000 individuals. The total height of the main tower is 131 feet. The height of the front bell towers is a total of 70 feet. Inside at its tallest, the main ceiling is 55 feet tall. The initial funds for the building of the Great Auditorium came from donations in August of 1893. At that time, rallies were held at the old auditorium and the ministers of the day, including Elwood Stokes, President of the Camp Meeting Association, whose seated statute is out front of the Great Auditorium gave powerful speeches that stirred listeners to contribute over $76,000 to the project.

The raising of the giant steel truss that holds the roof and all the main structural elements was completed without the assistance of modern cranes. Ginpoles, long masts were used to hoist the heavy metal monsters in place. Like a giant erector set, the Auditorium grew from the top down, fed with the religious fervor of the workers. They knew they were building a Great Auditorium. One to survive the ages. They could hear the voices which would soon be lifted in praise of God and with their fervor, the job was done in a mere three months. It is the centerpiece of the Grove. The ground around it is consecrated with the thousands of souls who have come here on their personal pilgrimage. The poor and the famous as well have found their way here.

The Great Auditorium was the Ed Sullivan Show of the Nineteenth Century. The roster of guest entertainment and famous people, both visitors and speakers to the Great Auditorium has never been completely compiled. The famous of their day, now almost completely forgotten, enthralled crowds with their songs, their words, and their music. What they all have in common is a middle American acceptability to hard and fast Methodists who shun alcohol, bad language, and off color remarks. Imagine seeing Enrico Caruso in a recital belting out arias from famous operas. A ticket to the event would have been $1.50. You could have seen Lawrence Tibbett or Lilly Pons or Nellie Melba or Jerome Hines, all from the world of opera. Or famous movie stars like Jeanette McDonald and Nelson Eddie. The Auditorium also brought concert artists like Efrem Zimbalist and Jascha Heifetz.

The stage has also been graced by the superstars of American Band music: Arthur Pryor and John Philip Sousa. To this day, around the 4th of July, a Sousa concert is presented by the Allentown Band. For that evening, it is again 1910. Sousa often appears himself in his marching band uniform with gold epaulettes and big gold buttons, bearded, waving his wooden baton.

The orchestras and bands are too numerous to count but the New Jersey Symphony Orchestra still makes the Auditorium its summertime home for its series. So too did Duke Ellington and Fred Waring and the

Preservation Hall Jazz Band.

More contemporary visitors have got to visit with Peter Paul and Mary as they sang, "If I had a Hammer" and "Puff the Magic Dragon" or to listen to Tony Bennett wail about the City by the Bay. If they were lucky, Neil Sedaka would sing "Calendar Girl" for them and meet them afterwards out in the open space outside the Auditorium with an impromptu autograph signing session where some little sixteen year old got a program signed, "To Liz, Happy Birthday, Sweet Sixteen, Love, Neil Sedaka."

It is all quite fitting for the singing and dancing to be brought to the Auditorium. The Methodist religion is the singing religion, Sunday sermons punctuated with hymns that have been sung through the decades. Spectacular choir festivals are also arranged in the Auditorium. Their singing, like the voices of angels, reaches high to the heavens and reverberates along Ocean Pathway. Often, they can be heard practicing on a summer day by bathers sprawled on the beach.

Famous speakers and explorers all have taken the podium enthralling Ocean Grovers with their stories of faraway lands. Admiral Byrd, with his stories of Antarctica and Lowell Thomas, one of the greatest travelers and radio personalities who has ever lived.

Andrew Carnegie, William Jennings Brian, Helen Keller. Will Rogers in his famous cowboy attire twirled his rope on stage and told homey stories that fit well with the Methodist message.

And the Presidents have come also. Ulysses S. Grant's sister lived in the Grove. He was a frequent visitor as well as lecturer at the Auditorium. James A. Garfield, William McKinley, Teddy Roosevelt, William Howard Taft, Woodrow Wilson, and even the beloved conservative himself, Richard Nixon, have all heard the thunder of applause echo in the massive wooden structure. Most every New Jersey Governor has put in an appearance at least once during their term to address the thousands assembled.

Then, of course, there is the Great Organ of the Auditorium. It is the first and most famous organ built by Robert Hope Jones. The organ was built at a cost of $27,000 and was first played on July 3, 1908 before an audience of 8,000 people. Recitals were given daily. In 1969, the organ was rebuilt and enlarged. The organ itself is housed in four concrete chambers behind the choir loft. The chamber walls are fourteen inches thick and twenty-five feet high. The great wooden ceiling of the Auditorium itself acts as a sounding board. The organ uses wind pressures generated by two huge blowers in the basement. The largest pipe of the organ is thirty-two feet long and three feet across at the top. There are 1,312 pipes. Patrons could hear the massive organ played in recitals by famed resident organists which included Will C. McFarlane, Clarence Reynolds, Harold Fix, Clarence Kohlman, Josephine Eddowes, Beverly Davis, Jon Quinn, Robert Carwithen, and the current organist, Gordon Turk, who has served in that function since 1974. It was the first musical director, Tali Esen Morgan who first contracted to have the Hope Jones organ built for the Auditorium. Today, free organ recitals are a common occurrence. Those strolling by the Auditorium can hear Gordon Turk preparing for one of his many organ recitals. To sit in the audience is to have one's innards vibrated to the massive resonating chords of the powerful pipes. One can imagine massive blasts of air streaming from the basement up through metal tubes that are the heart and soul of the instrument. Looking upon the stage, the large metal pipes become part of the Victorian background of the exposed metal truss and fine woodwork of ceiling and floor.

At the front of the Auditorium is the phrase in lettering six feet tall, "Holiness to the Lord. So be ye Holy." And the large centerpiece is a giant American flag crowned with electric lights which, by a flip of the switch, create the electronic illusion of waving in the breeze. There is no audience that is able to resist the patriotic surge of the stirring sight of this auditorium monument appearing to wave indoors in a patriotic light show. A recent debate grew over removing the old flag in favor of a safer more electronically controllable device. It was safety that eventually won out. The thought that the super dry hundred year old wooden structure having a possible faulty electrical connection reduce it to ashes led even the most staunch supporter of the old flag to agree to its removal and updating with a modern version. During services, the flag is replaced by a twelve foot cross.

The last time you saw an usher was probably at your local movie house when a kid with a flashlight helped you locate the car keys that fell out of your pocket. In the Great Auditorium, the ushers have developed into a drill team that not only greets the Sunday congregation but maintains order at the huge secular activities that are conducted there as well. These men wear a uniform of white pants, white shoes, white shirt, tie, and blue sports coat. At the appointed moment during Sunday services, the congregation is treated to a musical march of the Auditorium ushers written by Auditorium organist, Clarence Kohlman, during his period of reign from 1924 until 1945. At that time, the Auditorium capacity was listed at ten thousand. Perhaps Kohlman got the melody for the march by listening to a Sousa concert or from the calliope across the way in Asbury Park that played turn of the century melodies as the Great Ferris Wheel spun slowly in the ocean breezes. The ushers march to the syncopated sounds as they move quickly among the congregation collecting baskets of donations from the faithful which help defray the cost of maintaining the Great Auditorium. Dick Furbeck had been the President of the Auditorium ushers from 1990 to 1996. He has spent forty-three years in Ocean Grove. He came to town as a boy, helping Grandma with her place in the Grove. Like many of the youth, he and his family lived in one of the hundreds of tents that still survive today. He recounts stories of how a "good night" to his parents was met by good nights up and down the tent row. These tents with large canvas fronts became the living area and bedroom facilities. Heat is provided by a well-placed electric blanket. Young kids like Dick Furbeck went to sleep with the sound of concerts ringing in their ears from the Great Auditorium only yards away.

I live in the house of one of the former secretaries of the ushers, Dick Borden. In fact, when speaking about where I live in town, most people simply refer to my house as Dick Borden's house, who lived their peaceably with his wife, Catherine. The ushers are a men's group, but so that women would not be denied, there is the Ladies Auxiliary of the Auditorium ushers. They are responsible for revenue raising themselves; wonderful plant and book sales, and not to be missed, marvelous and enticing bake sales held beneath the Pavilion during the spring and summer.

Children play an essential role in the fabric of the Great Auditorium. It is these young impressionable minds that will become the Methodist leaders of tomorrow. Youth Groups which focus on music and fun with a message of clean living have been the hallmark of their life in the Grove. The Great Auditorium, as well as Thornley Chapel, play heavily in the life of any kid whose parents see fit to have them exposed to a religious upbringing. Out front of the Beersheba well in the park, you will see that the Youth Temple has once again risen. With over a million dollars in contributions, this steel and wooden structure integrated in the Victorian architecture of the square, houses the meeting place for the youth of Ocean Grove. A hundred years ago, a similar Youth Temple served their needs on the same site. During the summer, Thornley Chapel just down the street is the site of the Children's Daily Bible School. It is where the Music Program for kids is conducted. Many of the kids who get their exposure through the Thornley Chapel go on to become leaders in the Camp Meeting Association and the town itself. It is impossible to separate the religious foundation of Ocean Grove from the contemporary life of the town. There may be some who come here solely for the sand and surf but most understand that the Grove is much more, a system that produces devout people devoted to God and country. A place where they receive specific instructions on how to live in an otherwise very confusing and tumultuous world. The old Youth Temple was taken from the Grove in a spectacular fire, and the new promises a place for kids to gather for the next hundred years.

Believe it or not, the kids of Ocean Grove have not always been angels. At one time, their rebellious ways led the Camp Meeting Association to foster a group called the Roosevelt Rough Riders. Teddy Roosevelt had become popular for his charge with his own Rough Riders up San Juan Hill in Cuba. The Camp Meeting Association sponsored a similar group for children. Little boys and girls dressed in uniforms imitating the garb of Roosevelt's own Rough Riders. They trained under the summer sun, performed drills and received the most important ingredient of all, discipline, under the loving eyes of their leaders. These days, the Rough Riders are gone and in their place are summer plays that kids put on for auditorium crowds. They practice all summer in their roles of Cinderella or Beauty and the Beast and other stories from the past that carry with them important messages to guide them on life's road. The Youth Temple is approaching completion as you read this book. Soon kids of the Twenty-First Century will take their place among the tens of thousands of kids who have passed through the Youth Temple and the Great Auditorium over the last hundred years enjoying religious services, the camaraderie and the guidance that the Grove supplies.

The Grove is enjoying a Renaissance, as is the Camp Meeting Association and religious revival itself. Baby boomers lost in the sea of affluence at the price of the loss of personal freedom flock to the Auditorium as a pilgrimage in search of salvation. Others will come solely for the entertainment. Some will just lounge outside on the grassy lawn in their lawn chairs, listening to the events inside behind the huge sliding barn doors with stained glass windows. This summer, like summers before, there is a full schedule of both religious and secular events in the Great Auditorium. Numerous organ recitals are scheduled from June to August. Most of these are at Saturday noon and Wednesday evenings at 7:30. They feature the resident organist, Gordon Turk, as well as organists from around the world.

On Sunday afternoons, light music is provided by the Auditorium soloists, all opera stars in residence: Monica Zagler, soprano; Melora Love, mezzo-soprano; Ronald Naldi, tenor; Kevin Short, bass-baritone; David Arnold, baritone and guest soloist. On Wednesday evenings at 8:00 during July and August, the Ocean Grove Summer Band presents Pavilion boardwalk of popular seaside music. These are free concerts.

And of course, there is the entertainment schedule at the Auditorium itself. Starting on

May 26 with the Orchestra of St. Peter by the Sea,
June 2: Manhattan Rhythm Kings,
June 9: Doo Wop,
June 16: Broadway and Love,
June 30: The Allentown Bank Celebrates the Fourth,
July 7: Jerry Vale,
July 14: The Tommy Dorsey Orchestra,
July 21: Trinity,
July 28: The Glenn Miller Orchestra,

August 4: Three Dog Night,
August 11: Neil Sedaka,
August 18: Alexandria Harmonizers,
August 25: Peter, Paul and Mary,
September 1: A Second Doo Wop Show,
September 8: Orchestra of St. Peter by the Sea.

Religiously, as there have been for years, there will be daily Bible Study every Monday through Saturday morning from 9 a.m. to 10 a.m. at the Bishop Jane's Tabernacle which is the Victorian building next door to the Great Auditorium itself.

For 2001, the 132nd Annual Camp Meeting will begin on August 5 to August 12. This is a spiritual period where the faithful come from all over the country and the world to participate in intensified religious observance with the great preachers of the day, including the Rev. Dr. Tony Compolo, the Rev. Dr. Charles Killian, and the Rev. Dr. Umberto Alfaro.

The Auditorium also hosts a classical series on:

July 5: Horn and Pipes,
July 12: Clarinet, Cello, and Piano,
July 19: Violin and Piano,
July 26: Flute, Cello, and Piano,
August 2: Piano Duo.
And of course, beginning in June, regular Sunday worship at the Auditorium at 10:30 a.m.

The beach is respectfully closed until services are concluded at 12:30 p.m.

CHAPTER 10

The Queen

The Queen simply blew over, not the victim of fire, or a gigantic metal wrecking ball, or a storm of notable vengeance. It just leaned over and died, like the old lady she was. Tired. Lifeless. Her innards removed for restoration and weakened in the process, she stood for months waiting renaissance, empty and barren to the walls.

I had ridden my bicycle past her just the night before. I could see the ocean and stars through the holes in her walls, they having been torn away to the beams that held up her Victorian roof. The porches sagged to a "v" shape, where once patrons rocked in ladder back chairs to the rhythm of the ocean waves. In the morning, there she was, on her side, boards twisted and broken, shoved into a slanted pyramid of rubble, as if she had been slapped by a giant's hand that caused her to fall and slip sideways. No smoke or fire or dust, just there on her side, the way sailors say old ships go to the bottom. Gently, without a sound, in slow motion.

"Daddy, where's our room?" Liz said.

"Over there, somewhere," I said.

A moment of silence for the remains of our favorite tower room. It had been the place Liz saw Rapunzel weave her hair and spin her gold, and where the prince had scaled the walls to free her from the clutches of the mean king who sought her hand. Now it was just a pile of sticks with pipes and slate shingles broken on the ground.

"What happened, Daddy?" said Liz.

"It got tired of just standing there without people inside, so it just laid down for a rest," I said.

In a few days she was gone. Yellow plastic caution tape like they use at crime scenes had been strung about to keep the curious away. Tiny pieces of porch rails became souvenirs and a brick or two ended up in someone's patio. But that was all. The wreckers and trucks came and soon only a depression in the ground where the foundation had stood was left. The Ocean Pride, next door, bore scars of the Queen's demise, missing a shingle or two, a rain spout perhaps, but no real damage. The Pride's south windows were bathed in morning light, after being blocked for more than a hundred years by the Queen. The Lluch family rents its fourteen rooms, as they have for the last twenty-two years. During the Queen's day, it was a mere dwarfed cousin, as the Queen was the white gleaming sentinel on the corner.

We had rented the same room in the Queen most weekends for the last few summers. It was in the tower that looked out over the ocean. It had five windows so you could look in every direction and a floor that made you walk up hill to bed. It always passed Liz's toilet paper test. She would lie in her bed near the flower papered wall and gently place the roll on the floor. It would zig and zag to the exact spot in the corner. She would do it a dozen times, each time letting out a satisfied girlish giggle. There were three rooms in the tower. I would ask Howie, the owner, to hold the top floor for us. It was like staying in a castle high above the street. I would set up my telescope on the fire escape and during the day we would watch happy people on boats, swigging beer from Budweiser cans, who only occasionally glanced away from pretty companions in tiny bikini bathing suits to see if any fish had found their way to one of the lines overboard. At night, the moon would rise right out of the ocean, yellow and full sometimes. The telescope would be Liz's science lesson for the evening. I'd get the lunar mountains and craters in focus for her to view, as I held her firmly out one of the big windows. When it was time for her to sleep, we would tuck her in and I would go across Ocean Avenue to sit on the wooden bench. The kiss of the sea breeze would develop snapshots of the day's family memories.

"Pull me up, Daddy. Here comes a big wave," she'd say.

I would hold her little arms and, in one motion, swing her away from the crest of the tiny wavelet, as it barely touched her knees. Over and over in the sparkling sea that looked like a broken mirror in the sun, she'd wiggle and squirm in delight with each jump.

"Again, Daddy, do it again."

I would forget the awful drive down the Parkway in bumper to bumper traffic, Liz playing waitress to pass the time.

"What'll you have tonight, sir?"

"Can I take your order, please?"

And she would fold back the little book with carbon paper, like real waitresses used to, and start scribbling words like, "sup," and "chikan," and "riz," followed by "$24.95, plus tax." If I want a good cry, I can pull them out of a box up in the attic, where I stuck them maybe twenty years ago, and flash back to the car drive.

I was always amazed at her lady-like qualities at four years old. She talked to Howie and Helen, the Queen's owners, about her week and asked what they had done and if the weather was good and if many people had come to sit on the porch and rock. They treated her special, too. She, with her blond curls, blue eyes, and pink skin, not a trace of my Mediterranean heritage. She wore big plastic, bluish framed glasses. She had a condition called lazy-eye and with corrective lenses, we had been told by the time she was eight or so, her slightly crossed eyes would be normal. They made her bookish looking, like a tiny child librarian. She'd pose for pictures with her half toothed smile or belt out the tunes from "Annie," her favorite show.

"The sun will come out, tomorrow; so you've got to hang on till tomorrow." In the middle of a drizzly afternoon in the big living room of the hotel, aged guests would clap and egg her on.

Helen photographed her in a pensive pose, sitting on the wooden steps that led off of Ocean Pathway to the porch and the big glass doors of the hotel and gave me the black and white photo blown up, poster size, for my birthday. The sun is shining off the frame of her glasses and the slyest of smiles, like the Mona Lisa's, suggest all the youth and potential of a child of that age.

I would rock for hours on the big porch with friends I had made from the weekly trips. Hillary was an executive in the city. He was a regular, too. Knew everyone, but came and went solitary, reading a big thick novel by someone I had never heard of. We'd compare notes about life and work. I confided my feelings in him, though I hardly knew him at all. It was safe to do. He neither criticized nor judged. We just rocked together, slowly, along with maybe twenty other people on the porch.

The Queen was built in 1886 with a narrow front door facing the ocean. But its five stories went the entire length of the building, seventy-five feet along Ocean Pathway. It made a reviewing stand for the vast open green in front of the Auditorium at one end, and the boardwalk pavilion at the other. That open space, with the sidewalk for strollers in the center, had a sign posted at both its ends: "No Bicycles." Straight forward.

But, notwithstanding the warning, as afternoon sashays to twilight, dads were out there giving their kids their first bicycle riding lesson as moms watched from rockers, waiting the signal to change places. Liz got her first wobbly lesson there, too; me running along side.

"Don't let go, Daddy. Don't," she said.

I, of course, had long since let go and she was cruising along just fine until an aluminum light pole interrupted her ride. Down, with scraped elbows and knees, she went. "My elbow feels sticky," came through watery eyes and a choking sigh. But she got up and went on her way quickly, like most kids. Invincible.

Howie greeted guests from a long counter in the corner of the foyer just inside the glass doors carved out of the space beneath the steps. Behind him, on brass hooks, were the room keys lined up for the sixty rooms the hotel had for rent. His father had owned the Queen, as had his uncle before him, and he had returned to continue the family tradition. Young, filled with pep, he handled the guests with the charm of a lounge singer, crooning fond hellos and see ya's to little old ladies who would insist on renting the same room every week. They were his guests and friends, as well. They would bring him news of the goings on in New York City, or North Jersey, or where ever.

"Duty calls, to use a pun," he'd say, carrying an old-fashioned rubber plunger up the creaky third floor steps. Under his breath, "Sixty rooms of gloom, never any rest."

The hotel, in its heyday, saw guests ranging from former Presidents such as Teddy Roosevelt, in a straw skimmer and spats, to the parents of the Chairman of General Electric, proper and sedate, to preachers at the Auditorium working on sermon notes, and just plain folks, oblivious to the pedigree of fellow patrons, they may be sharing the porch with.

The living room was filled with Victorian wood trimmed, overstuffed chairs in deep magenta, worn thread bare by the comings and goings of people over the years. Some would sit in the same chair for most of the weekend, never stepping foot outside, just enjoying the peace of the long wide room and the sternly painted Victorian portraits of ancestors looking down from their wire perches, along pink satin covered walls. Howie would leave the small front door and the two large glass side doors open, and the breeze would fill the parlor with ocean air conditioning.

On busy weekends, the hotel was alive with bags and luggage lined up to be carried to seaside rooms. Visitors of all ages would find their way to the porch rockers to glide away evenings effortlessly; their chatter in whispers barely audible would be broken by an occasional belly-sized laugh and then all would be quiet again.

Each day and night melted together. Eventually, the faces of the guests all resembled each other staying in rooms that were tiny and musty smelling from years of mold and mildew.

Throughout the Victorian period, hotels blossomed in the Grove to handle the ever expanding tourist trade. Gone now are some of the largest and most fancy. Victims of fire or bankruptcy.

When the Queen was young and the streets were dirt and horses were stabled near to where my present house stands on Abbott Avenue, the Grove was already a tourist resort and curious articles appeared in publications of the day. The *Scientific American* of September 28, 1889, carried a front page story about the Grove's attempt to harness the ocean waves. With color illustration, the article explained how a heavy swinging gate affixed to piers at the water level would be battered back and forth with the waves. Each shove of the tide would cause the gate to push a shaft into a long metal piston. The resulting pressure would drive water from a well in the sea bed up a forty-foot run of pipe to a large wooden cistern over a pavilion on the boardwalk. That accumulated water would be used to salt spray the town's streets. With the aid of the device, forty thousand gallons could be drawn from the sea each day without a motor of any kind. Perhaps, future ambitious visitors to the Grove will see the wisdom in such a system to run turbines for the creation of pollution-free electricity.

In the 1970's and 1980's with rooms to let and few tourists, some hotel owners made contracts with State Social Service providers to house discharged mental patients deemed safe enough to be released to the community. With the 90's and economic prosperity, most turned them out in favor of well-heeled tourists who could pay the freight, unblinkingly. But, during those earlier times, the stage was set for the more colorful characters who continue to live in the Grove.

The Friday night dinner special at Stokes Hall up Ocean Pathway was $4.95. It included roast beef, potatoes, vegetable, iced tea, and a piece of one of the guest's leftover birthday cakes from a few days before. The waitress, in a red lopsided wig with strong masculine hands and powerful calves and thighs, would try to ratch-up a man's voice several octaves for the occasion. I remember Liz asking me a simple question that caused me pause.

"Daddy, is that a lady?" she said.

"Yes, Honey," and left it at that.

I am sure many people have their story about their stay in the Grove. The combination of sweet surprise and plain disbelief. It is certainly not the same as anywhere else I have ever been.

The Queen is just a white wooden-clabbered ghost and its guests have been absorbed some into other hotels, and others into the very fabric of the Grove.

My little girl is now twenty-two, living on her own, hardly ever riding a bicycle anymore. She did not become a waitress, despite all the practice she got taking orders.

I watch visitors, from time to time, walk by the vacant lot on Ocean Pathway, ignoring the few broken bricks that still protrude. They can see only the shadows cast by nearby buildings on the spot where once stood the grand Queen Hotel.

CHAPTER 11

Main Avenue

In their quest to keep the Grove separate and apart from the real world, the Methodist founders took great pain to establish Main Avenue practically in the center of their square mile of peaceful heaven. Unlike bordering communities, which jumped on the chance to have Route 71 be their Main Street, Ocean Grovers were content to establish that kind of Main Street designed to serve the immediate community and none other. So it was then no accident that Main Avenue grew from the beachfront, where the bronze winged angel statue once stood in a perpendicular line clear to the stone gate pillars across which the Sunday closing chains were strung. By this design, all homes in the Grove were easily walkable to obtain groceries, clothes, do banking, and other shopping. In the last ten years, Main Avenue has grown into a tourist attraction that caters to the summertime buying urges of visitors as well as serving the needs of the 4,000 year round residents of the Grove.

It wasn't so long ago that a parking space along Main Avenue was available twelve months of the year. These days with the clamor of tourists, many from New York City, realizing that the Grove is but an hour and a half away, those parking spaces are filled year round. But locals still come to Main Avenue by foot and of course by bicycle and return carrying bags of local groceries and other goodies. A stroll up and back Main Avenue is a vacation must do, and it helps to know something about the shops on the way. Watch for traffic as you cross the street but take a walk with me now. We'll start at the eastern edge of the commercial district and walk west for a while.

On the corner of Central and Main Avenue was once the site of one of the most delectable bakeries this side of Avon-by-the-Sea, the Macaroon Shop. The large wooden swinging screen doors would let ocean breezes in to carry the smells coming from the trays and trays of magically prepared cookies and pastry delights all along Main Avenue. A morning coffee and a chocolate covered cookie, supplying enough sugar to kill any diabetic, was nonetheless a favorite A.M. appetizer. A.M., as in Amazing Macaroon. The swinging doors are gone now replaced by the metal glass, wired and secured entry way of the Provident Savings Bank. That's where Jimbo found his frozen turkey, by the way.

Just up the street is the flower shop owned for years by the Trouwborst family and now owned and operated by Cathy and Tom Rechlin, who in another life owned and ran the Sampler Inn. With mixed emotions,

Tom Rechlin had sold the Sampler and caved into Cathy's desires to get out from behind the cashier's desk and its endless parade of tourists and locals alike. Ted Trouwborst used to live down the street from me. He looked a little like the man who played the Wizard in the Wizard of Oz. He owned a thirty foot mobile home and would park out front of his house on Benson Avenue, which always told me that it would be time for another trip. On return, he would be over with his wife, Ella, to tell me of the different places he had visited on his tour. Ted's gone now and I miss his adventure stories. Ella and her two sons, Ted and Gary, still live in the Grove. They had tried to make a go of the flower shop themselves after Ted's death, but it wasn't long before they decided that it was time to give up the family business. The boys still work helping Tom, but the crazy hours and dealing with the public are no longer their problem. You can see stacks and stacks of fresh flowers, annuals, and perennials out front of the flower shop most days in the spring, summer, and fall. Cathy's added Ocean Grove signature clothing and tons of souvenirs to be purchased by the tourists.

Just a couple of doors up from the flower shop was Ocean Grove's only barber shop. It was a real time barber shop, where you could get your hair cut for a few dollars and at the same time learn all you needed to know about the local gossip, sports, politics, and religion. The barber shop is gone now, turned into a variety of stores including a 90's video store complete with racks and racks of DVD's, potato chips, and popcorn for the sit back and watch crowd.

Right next door is the Daily Grind. They've added American Bake Shop to the name and a bunch of tiny tables to sit and eat fabulous desserts. But at one time not too long ago, that was a narrow corridor of a place that bore only the name, the Daily Grind. It's there where local musicians would play out front much like they do during these summers. Probably the most famous of those entertainers are Frank Rafferty and Spring. These two local songwriters and performers, a modern Les Paul and Mary Ford, added flair and color to Main Avenue and often complaints by local neighbors, when their singing went beyond the ordinance of quiet time at 10:00 p.m.. Can you imagine a summer crowd wanting to tuck in at ten? Fans could get more of Frank, as he actually worked the coffee pumps and cappuccino machine during the day.

The Ballad of Frank Rafferty

Faster than a speeding bullet,
sweeter than the Cappo maker's whine,
look their on Kingsley ... it's a bird,
no, it's Frank on the way to the Grind.

What's that white thing,
hanging from his lips?

Hidden soon between his fingertips,
as he pours the daily sips.

To eager Ocean Grovers from every part can tell,
red eyed morning monsters, lured in by java's smell.
"Hey, what'll it be?"
"All right then."
Is the troubadour's upbeat way.
A twang of dreamer man or a double cream latte?
Frank is fearless no matter their every quirk.
He knows between his flannel
beats the heart of super jerk!

It was not always as you know,
not born to this it seems.
Who finds so quick a home
among the coffee creams?
Only one whose heart beats true,
can separate the grinds from the daily brew.

So ye dudes and chicks alike,
who wander in and seek the light.
Remember on the way to dreams,
the path is strewn with latte creams.
Some day we may look fondly on this humble bar,
and realize to ourselves .... jeez ...
we were jerked coffee by a star!

Spring reminds me of Sarah McLachlan with the face and voice of an angel. She does, in fact, do a number of church ceremonies in the area for pay. I have been privileged to have both of these artists as my friends. And of course, anyone interested in buying their CD's can ask anybody in the Grind about them. On many a winter day, Frank, Spring, Diane, and I sat in the tiny corner of the Grind as the morning sun came through the large stained glass window. Locals would trudge in to get their first espresso of the day and maybe listen to Frank belt out one of his latest tunes like "Evil Deli Girl." Great as these entertainers are, they are still waiting for that big break. Maybe as the Grove soars, local entertainers will be carried aloft with it.

Everybody's favorite store is Favorite Things, farther up the block. Harvey and Aida left a life in North Jersey to become one of the first "fancy" boutiques to move into town. Their expensive line of jewelry, knick knacks, and Ocean Grove memorabilia looked totally out of place years ago, but now one store has grown to three along the street, and shopaholics find hours of amusement among their wares for sale. If you're lucky, you'll get to meet Barbara, who may be one of the most beautiful women to live in the Grove. Her white skin, dewy blue eyes, and pursed red lips have always been a welcome addition to the corps of shopkeepers who have run the stores in the Grove over the last hundred years. You can find her either in Favorite Things or Ocean Grove Trading at the other end of the street, which was and still is the only hip clothing store in the Grove. I like to tell the story of the time I went in to see Barbara at the Trading Company on a day she was wearing a blue and white striped boating sweater. She looked like she had just stepped off the Presidential yacht. Standing behind the glass counter, she was dazzling to behold. A rather chubby woman realized that the outfit Barb was wearing was displayed on a nearby counter. Straining my peripheral vision to the max, I watched as she pulled and stretched the French boating top to fit her enormous frame. Quietly, she stepped into the fitting room and emerged looking more like a Russian submariner but she happily made her way to the front desk and payed for the expensive blouse.

Continuing up Main Avenue is the Main Avenue Deli. This place is near and dear to my heart, as it figures into my own arrival in the Grove. There have been many proprietors of what is now called Randel's Deli. At one time, large painted letters on the window declared it to be the Main Avenue Deli and Mattie Carrera and his wife, Susan, the proprietors. Mattie is a kind of mustached teddy bear with a heart of solid gold, soft brown eyes, and the friendly disposition that made the Grove a special place for me. Coffee, breakfast sandwiches, lunch sandwiches, and a small catering business on the side is how Mattie ran the deli for years.

After years of holing up in rented rooms at the

Queen Hotel, I decided to look for a little house in the Grove. I eventually found a place for sale by owner, but was concerned that I didn't know the neighborhood. It was a tiny one bedroom house, but it had a fabulous garage, and in town, at that time, as now, such an item was priceless. I went to see Mattie, who was good friends with Howie and Helen, the then owners of the Queen Hotel on Ocean Avenue, now gone from Ocean Avenue. Howie worked with Mattie and they had been friends for years.

"Matt, I found this cute little place. It has a garage and I need to know what you think," I said.

"So where is the place?" Mattie quizzed.

"It's on the corner of Abbott and Benson. A little tiny gray house."

"Oh, I see. Well, there could be some problems with the neighbors."

At that time there was a nasty four family across the street that was down at the heel and a number of rental units nearby.

"The real problem is the one on Webb," Mattie said.

"Is it really?" I responded, "It looks like a fine place."

"Yeah, but the neighbors are noisy; they've gotta couple kids; the guy goes off to work before six in the morning, and there is this constant smell of tomato sauce and pies baking in the oven."

"Funny, I hadn't noticed a thing. It looked perfectly safe to me. By the way, Matt, how do you know so much about that corner?"

"Simple," he said, "I live there."

That made up my mind instantly and Matt and I have been friends and neighbors for the last twenty years. He doesn't own the Main Avenue Deli anymore but still does catering from time to time. New fellows took over the deli and they eventually sold to the present owners that run Randel's.

No trip to Ocean Grove would be complete without stopping at the Shell Shop. When I was a kid, there was a five and ten cent store in Lodi that set out tiny toys and junk for kids, as well as all of the other notions and novelties that adults would buy from zippers to carpet tacks and hammers. They were all just laid out on counters with glass partitions which could be moved to vary the size of the space needed for the articles for sale. That's what the Shell Shop looks like. It looks almost like the sea simply washed up thousands and thousands of shells into neat piles for display. When my daughter, Liz, was a little girl, she loved going into the Shell Shop and looking at the different shells from around the world. I confess, I've always liked going in there myself. If it's not just a shell you're after, you could get a lamp, a wishing well, a shell studded mirror or jewelry box to take home.

    Nearby was the Dolphin, a local hamburger joint for many years which went upscale by adding a piano in the 80's. Dinner was offered and it was, perhaps, one of the first restaurants to begin catering to the new crowd that came to the Grove. This was years before the Raspberry Café and Moonstruck hit the dining scene. More about them later. The old Dolphin is now Captain Jack's, which caused a little bit of a stir since Jack Green's dad is the President of the Camp Meeting Association and rumors spread that the restaurant was permitting, heaven forbid, the imbibing of alcoholic beverage on the premises. Most of the restaurants in town look the other way when patrons B.Y.O. even though the Grove remains dry and no matter your thirst, neither wine nor beer can be purchased anywhere.

Farther down the street is the Kitch and Kaboodle. Frankly, I thought this store would close two hours after it opened. Selling 60's stuff, it had the look of a permanent garage sale, but the ability to know the tourist trade has led the owners to do well in selling anything from used quilts to cookbooks. We've reached the top of the commercial district, and it's time to cross the street.

Crossing the street at the top of Main Avenue, you are taken aback by the large Victorian building which houses Tina's Gift Shop. It is the old C.C. Clayton homestead, built in 1884. It was the grandest home in the Grove and cost $14,000 to build: marble floors in the vestibule, carved chestnut double front doors, beveled glass interior doors and a winding cherry wood staircase. If that were not enough, stained glass windows by Louis Tiffany grace the first and second floors and the chandelier in the main entrance is said to be 14 Karat gold plated. Tina is the first lady of restoration in the Grove. It was her vision many years ago that the Grove would, in fact, come back. She has operated a gift shop in Asbury Park for years. But here in the Grove, her sap green paint and okra yellow highlighting can be credited for starting it all. Tina can't fool me. I know who she really is. Tiny metal frame glasses, white hair, rosy cherub cheeks, and all those toys "for good little girls and boys." I recognized it the first time I ever met her when I strolled into her building when still under construction. Don't let her tell you any different. Just take a look around her store and you'll know for sure. The goodies that all kids dream of. Victorian dolls, lace table clothes and napkins, precious jewelry, stones, and a vast collection of assorted vases. This is the stuff that tourism is built on. I have no idea how much money any of these establishments make on Main Avenue these days, but whether it is sunny and warm or raining and miserable, the shoppers browse among the piles of inventory seductively placed on glass and wood shelves in places like Tina's. If you're looking for that special china tea cup imported from merry old London, I'm sure Tina can accommodate you. If your kids are dying to have a Victorian stroller with a porcelain faced doll, this is the place for you. This is the sunny side of the street as well. So those few boyfriends, husbands, and lovers who aren't curious about the historical Clayton House and its architecture can lollygag outside while the women go inside and give the plastic money a chance to do its thing.

Right after Tina's is Whippersnapper's, a shop filled with more tourist stuff. Not too long ago, it was the office of Gannon Construction. They moved a couple of years ago to Route 71 right outside the gates.

In the 1860's, tradesmen wore handlebar mustaches and wide flat brimmed straw hats and worked in sweat soaked, cotton-collared shirts, their skin burned a permanent red bronze from twelve hour days in the sun. The Gannon boys, Bill and Elaine's sons, are modern tradesmen, barrel-chested, in tan cargo shorts with heavy construction boots, t-shirts, and baseball caps. They have repaired, renovated, and built so many houses in Ocean Grove that their fingerprints could be found on most every doorknob in town. Builders. Plumbers. Playing charity volleyball on their plot of vacant land on the corner of Webb and Ocean Avenues, where now is rising the Grove's only steel frame house. No wood at all. Eighty thousand pounds of gray steel girders, thirty thousand pounds of rebar steel spikes, in tons of poured concrete, all designed to hold a thirty-five thousand gallon swimming pool on the roof, up thirty-four feet, eleven and three quarter inches to be exact.

Watching that building go up with iron workers, fearlessly sliding down the exposed steel shafts between floors like firemen on a slick metal pole, one can almost see ghosts of Victorian tradesmen, smiling down approvingly at their efforts.

The boys lost their dad on Memorial Day 2000, so with plans sketched by "kid" brother, Billy, on a napkin, brothers Paul, Matt, and Mark may be building a fitting memorial to their father, designed to last a thousand years.

Walking east, while not a tourist attraction in its own right, the most venerable office of Century 21 Real Estate deserves mention. This is the business the Huizenga family built. Ray, Chris, and Gary deserve much credit for getting the real estate market to move in the Grove. When buildings were selling for $50,000 and they couldn't be given away, it was the Century 21 people that saw the advantage of importing buyers from New York City and beyond. Convincing friends that this Valhalla by the beach would some day rise as the Hamptons did in Long Island. It is thanks to them and the other real estate agents in town that the Grove has been transformed from its quiet Methodist beginnings to the aspiring tourist Mecca that most likely has brought you here in the first place. Once you've stared and fantasized about the pictures of houses for sale out front of the real estate office, continue marching east. You will soon pass two brick bank buildings which only in the last several years acquired ATM facilities. You may need a visit to the ATM if you've made reservations to eat at Moonstruck a few doors down.

Ah, Moonstruck. New York Times Four Star restaurant, long lines, fancy dishes. Given any particular summer evening and the BMW, Mercedes, and Volvo owners crowd Main Avenue waiting an opportunity to sit on plastic chairs until one of Luke or Howard's table managers can get them a seat inside. Luke and Howard are both local guys who have parleyed their kitchen acumen and solid business sense into the Grove's most successful business. Their first business, the Raspberry Café across the street, had become the most popular breakfast place in town. Serving dinner as well in cramped quarters eventually led to the opening of Moonstruck across the street. Now, all is success. Vintage automobiles, well-tended gardens, and a house overlooking the lake where Stokes himself resided for a time. The Moonstruck restaurant was preceded by a pizza joint run by fellows from Brooklyn. Where now sit tables where dinner can run a hundred dollars or more, was a big metal pizza oven manned by people who looked more like extras from the Soprano series.

Don't wait too long to have that special dinner here at Moonstruck as the restaurant is to move to Asbury Park in the next year with dining facilities and, a very un-Ocean Grove bar for patrons overlooking Wesley Lake.

The imposing bell tower in the center of town housing the big clock face was once the offices of the Camp Meeting Association. On the verge of falling into disrepair, it was fortunately turned into luxury condominiums many years ago. On the first floor is the Ocean Grove Post Office, complete with wooden plank floor and old-fashioned slide glass windows with metal bars that keep patrons at a safe distance. For all of its renovation, the Post Office still retains a 1950's character. Post men and women have the look of contentment as they walk along tree lined streets under the summer sun being paid for what tourists do at a couple hundred dollars a day.

Don't overlook Freedman's Bakery. And if you are strolling on Friday, grab an apple turnover. They are scrumptious. Nothing is actually baked in this bakery. It's all brought in from Freedman's main bakery shop in Belmar on Route 71. Nonetheless, the offerings are usually fresh and under the careful and watchful eye of Don, a most curious store manager. His brand of sarcastic humor first thing in the morning sets the tone for the bargain coffee and roll at a $1.25. Just do not commit the mortal sin of expecting change of a twenty dollar bill before 9:00 a.m. By the way, if you can hold out until 4:00 p.m., the baked goodies go on a 40% sale. Early in the morning, this is a frequent destination for the more colorful personalities along Main Avenue.

Next door is the small former office of the real estate firm of Bronson and Blair. Stu Blair died recently. He lived over on Inskip Avenue in a small one-story ranch. I knew Stu Blair well. He dutifully took me about the town in the early 80's looking at small cottages and tried to convince me as to why I would not be interested in owning any of them. He had suggested Bradley Beach as a likely alternative. I don't think he believed me when I told him I was a Christian. Who would lie about such a thing?

Stu Blair kept a wad of five by seven index cards held together by an elastic band. This was the forerunner of the Pentium computer database spreadsheet analysis provided by Excel. When houses would sell, Stu would simply make notes on each of the individual cards, updating them accordingly. He could trace the lineage of a house back a hundred years. He'd be able to tell buyers the renovations and changes the last owner had made or four owners before him. He was brilliant. Twinkly blue eyes, a firm gaze, and a wry sense of humor.

Walk farther east. The gas pumps are now gone from out front of Howard Smith Hardware Store. I imagine their leaky tanks are still sitting somewhere under the sidewalk. When I first came to the Grove, the Howard Smith Hardware Store was, in fact, owned by Howard Smith. It was the kind of place you could buy a single bolt. These days, Dave runs the Ace Hardware Store. It's a modern version of the old-fashioned 50's hardware store. It's one of those stores where screws and bolts come prepackaged in nice cardboard boxes. Dave's wife has started an antique business and you can leave the clutter of the main floor to the restoration enthusiasts and spend some time upstairs among the accumulated Victoriana offered for sale. I am sure if you ask nicely, Dave will sell you a single bolt and a single screw. He'll also rent you a couple of beach cruiser bicycles for next to nothing a day. I envisioned going into that business myself years ago. Where the Kitch and Kaboodle store stands now, I had planned Kites and Bikes, a rental operation for both of them. You could rent a kite for a day; if you destroyed it, you owned it, if you returned it, it was simply a daily charge. Literally, it never got off the ground.

Note, as you walk, the cleaning establishment. You are looking at one of the last vestige of services offered to local residents. Sure, the tourists come here to get the homemade chocolate ice cream out of their cashmere sweaters, but at one time, it along with the other ordinary businesses in town, served the needs of locals only. Stroll by the small Victorian building, now Diane Turton Real Estate. My friend, Big Jim Hubbard, and I had planned to open a music studio and book store in that building. We missed the opportunity to buy it when it was $70,000. Arlene Fox got her hands on it and had to pay a great deal more. Arlene ran the Remax office there and just recently sold to Diane Turton. That building is probably worth close to half a million dollars now.

Last but not least, is Lenny Steen's chez d'oeuvre, Nagel's Pharmacy. At one time, Nagel's Pharmacy was a real drug store. Locals came in to have their prescriptions filled in this store with wooden plank floors and high tin ceiling. There was a small counter where you could get a soda and a sandwich. John Gross and his wife, Penny, were the pharmacists. John eventually got into politics and became Borough Administrator for Neptune Township and Penny moved to a pharmacy in Avon. The inventory on the shelves slowly dwindled and patrons found that the Rite-Aid and Eckerd establishments outside of the Grove could more quickly and reasonably respond to their pharmaceutical needs. Lenny Steen bought the building. It remained closed for over a year as meticulous renovations recreated the original 50's pharmacy as a restaurant serving breakfast, lunch, and dinner. Make sure to go in and see the dozens of old black and white photos that Lenny has arranged of the place from the 40's and 50's. The take-out window on Main Avenue literally serves tons of homemade ice cream and you can be serenaded by a street side piano player while you wait in the long line.

The commercial area that is Main Avenue continues to evolve, as barrels of flowers sit under light draped trees. Carefully selected Victorian trash cans have replaced fifty-five gallon drums emblazoned with the words, "God Likes Clean." Plans exist to redo the street lights on the Victorian scheme and to expand the commercial district itself. An atmosphere of Renaissance pervades the place.

Neglected in the 80's and 90's in favor of huge impersonal malls, people are returning to Main Streets. A trip to Main Avenue for tourists and locals alike offers a comfortable contact with other people; a friendly meeting place to see and be seen, and an opportunity to get the feel of the place.

The Great Auditorium is the heart and soul of the Grove, but Main Avenue is its skeleton and nerves.

CHAPTER 12

Timeless

I wrote these stories down for a selfish reason. Let me confess. I wanted to stop time. Grab change by the scruff of the neck and demand it stop twisting, pulling, and distorting every aspect of American life until it became unrecognizable to us "old timers," who remember how much better things *were*. Maybe all storytellers have that as one of their objectives, freezing people and places for memory's sake. These stories are an 8 x 10 glossy of what life was like in the Grove in the boom times of the late 90's and early 00's.

The Grove with arms now open wide embraces all people, Christians or not, fervent or passive: all are invited to enjoy its sunny shore. Even if it is Sunday. Gone are exclusive rights to any single religious group or belief; there is tolerance, liberation, and freedom for all. Sounds almost too good to be true, a society where, in its tiny domain, all is right as rain. That was what was intended, you know – a place to rest and restore the body and the spirit dedicated to the principle that achieving personal salvation is possible through righteous living.

The world is in a mess these days, and I run home to the Grove to find shelter from the storm of life. It seems too much like that day in the 60's when the "music died," when we were all frozen before black and white t.v. screens and felt the dull ache of true heartbreak. A sadness that runs to every part of the body and creeps in to even the most pleasant of thoughts and events. Always there, waiting to disrupt a happy life.

Sad times are not new to the Grove. It was founded soon after the end of the Civil War when Johnny came marching home, torn and tattered; it saw the Doughboys off to World War I to be ravaged by poison gas attacks; it sent the GI's to World War II and Korea, and Viet Nam with unspeakable hardships. But it remained, patiently waiting, ready to welcome them all home to a better world because of their efforts.

Krisanna's buttered roll seems sweeter to me as Robert tells me his boyhood memories of 1941 and how a friend's son left a small fluffy dog, like a canine dust mop, in his grandmother's care, as he went rushing off to war. The pup gave joy in time of sorrow, as the Grove has over the years.

The Grove celebrated the good times too. It saw the unification of the country from North to South and East to West, the extension of personal freedoms and equality for all in the Civil Rights Acts, the discovery of medicines that have cured diseases and extended life itself, and stunning achievements in outer space with wishes heard for peace and harmony from a man who took a giant step for mankind, standing beside Old Glory, unfurled in a windless world. Testament to Courage and Bravery.

Be sure the sun will shine again and the surf and sand will beckon. Hymns will be sung in the Great Auditorium, and people will continue to feel the lift and personal reward of trying to live a good and decent life. I wouldn't be surprised if attendance doubles at services next summer and each summer after that. Timeless.

With the summer season over, the big bench is back against the ticket window, waiting the early light of dawn with the "boys" sitting elbow-to-elbow. The walkers and runners cruise the boardwalk. Bicyclists come from as far as Sea Girt and Long Branch, miles away, as each day begins. The shelves are being restocked at the Pathway Market. Lovingly.

The Youth Temple has risen from its ashes and basketballs will soon be dribbled and tossed in waiting hoops and nets. Laughter and applause will rise as tiny kids do big acting jobs in *Beauty and the Beast* or *Cinderella,* making parents dewy-eyed with pride. Those kids will grow strong, replace their worn out elders, and carry on the ideals they have learned.

I know some things will endure, no matter the future and the changes it brings, like the joy of feeling connected to people and to a place. It's the key to happiness. Connection. We all need it. Crave it.

No, the Grove is not Utopia, despite the wishes of its founders. But it is on the right track and has been for more than one hundred years. Maybe visitors here now, more than ever, will take some of it home with them and share it with others and start their own Ocean Groves in their hearts with peace, tranquility, respect, and love for all, wherever they may live and whatever they may believe.

Kids and grandkids will want to know some day how things were in the old days.

"You know, grandpa, in the 00's," they'll say. We will have to tell them honestly; but exactly what, depends on us now.

Charter of the Ocean Grove Camp Meeting Association

"Recognizing the truth and beauty of the Scriptural declaration, 'The earth is the Lord's and the fullness thereof',"

"And being specially impressed with the propriety of having a portion of the land skirting the sea consecrated to sacred uses";

"We whose names are hereunto affixed, with a single eye to the Divine glory, and in humble dependence upon our Heavenly Father's aid, do hereby solemnly covenant together to use certain land, which has been providentially committed to our trust for those high and holy purposes."

Regulations Referred to in the Within Lease.

I. Every lot shall be subject to an Annual Assessment not to exceed Seven per cent, on the sum of One Hundred and Fifty Dollars, for the improvement and maintenance of the Camp Ground, to be paid within thirty days after notice given, if not so paid, one per cent, per month on the amount so due to be added until paid. If not paid within one year, the lease to be forfeited, and the improvements erected on said lot may be sold at Public sale by said Association, first giving notice of said sale for four weeks in a newspaper published in the County of Monmouth, and after deducting from the proceeds of said sale the amount of the aforesaid assessments, and the actual costs and expenses of the sale, the surplus, if any, to be paid to the Lessee, or his or her representatives.

II. No games or diversions of any kind, not approved by the Executive Committee of said Association, will be allowed on the Camp Meeting Ground, or any of the premises of the said Association, at any time.

III. The Association reserves the right at all times to use, lay out, and lease all lands not already laid out or designated, as streets or avenues.

Taken from my lease, the original is dated March 6, 1877 and signed by Elwood H. Stokes, President

Lease Indenture

Between Theodore M. David and the Ocean Grove Camp Meeting Association

The said Party of the Second Part shall not, and will not, at any time hereafter, without the written consent of the said Party of the First Part, their Successors or Assigns, use or occupy said demised premises, or any part thereof, or any building or other structure thereon, or suffer or permit the same or any part thereof, to be used or occupied as a Boarding House, or any mercantile or mechanical trade or purpose whatsoever, or in any other way or for any purpose, *except as a temporary residence and seaside resort, for and during the term commencing the fifteenth day of May, and ending with the thirtieth day of October of each year.*

Paragraph from Original Lease to my house, restricting use to the Camp Meeting summer season only.

"The Nation itself, with all its so called internal improvements, which, by the way are all external and superficial, is just such an unwieldy and overgrown establishment cluttered with furniture and tripped up by its own traps, ruined by luxury and heedless expense, by want of calculation and a worthy aim, as do a million households in the land; and the only cure for it, as for them, is in a rigid economy, a stern and more than Spartan simplicity of life, an elevation of purpose. It lives too fast, men think that it is essential that the Nation have commerce, and export ice and talk through a telegraph and ride thirty miles an hour, without a doubt whether they do or not; but whether we should live like baboons or like men is a little uncertain."

Henry David Thoreau
                      Walden1847

    Thoreau would have loved the Grove.

About the Author

Ted David is a father, lawyer, professor, and writer. He has over fifty publications in his field, including his professional book: *Dealing with the IRS*. His volume of warped poetry called "Here's Rhyme in Your Eye" is available on Amazon.com. A new Ocean Grove book called "Forgotten Ocean Grove" is in the works. He has loved the Grove for over thirty years.

This book is self-published to contain the outrageous costs and delays of seeking regular commercial publication.

If you have any comments or suggestions about this book, or to order additional copies, please contact me directly by e-mail at Tedd27@AOL.com. The book is now available on Amazon.com

Forgotten Ocean Grove

Did you know?

★ In 1869, it cost $40,000 to buy the entire tract of land that would become the Grove. Actually $39,368.35 for the 230 and 89/100 acres or $170.51 per acre.

★ The Great Auditorium was built in just 92 days and cost $76,000, $50,000 of which was raised in one Sunday, August 13, 1893.

★ The Great Auditorium has 1,145 light bulbs which are actually changed by being pulled up into the ceiling where they are replaced and then lowered back into position.

★ One cent toll bridges once existed over Wesley Lake between Ocean Grove and Asbury Park. In 1889, the total tolls were $3,413.74. 341,000 people had crossed over.

Soon to be released: ***Forgotten Ocean Grove*** **my next book filled with facts and trivia about Ocean Grove. It is an excellent little book to understand more about the town you love and a great companion for a self-guided walking tour of Historic Ocean Grove.**